CRUCIBLES OF CRIME
The Shocking Story of the
American Jail

PATTERSON SMITH REPRINT SERIES IN
CRIMINOLOGY, LAW ENFORCEMENT, AND SOCIAL PROBLEMS

PUBLICATION NO. 35: PATTERSON SMITH REPRINT SERIES IN
CRIMINOLOGY, LAW ENFORCEMENT, AND SOCIAL PROBLEMS

Crucibles
of Crime

THE SHOCKING STORY OF THE
AMERICAN JAIL

By

JOSEPH F. FISHMAN

Written in collaboration with

Vee Perlman

CENTRAL MISSOURI
STATE COLLEGE
Warrensburg

Montclair, New Jersey

PATTERSON SMITH

1969

Originally published 1923
Reprinted 1969 by
Patterson Smith Publishing Corporation
Montclair, New Jersey

SBN 87585-035-9

Library of Congress Catalog Card Number: 69-14923

CONTENTS

CHAPTER IV.

INSIDE THE CRUCIBLE

Kentucky Jails—A "Black Hole of Calcutta"—Special Features of Bowling Green — Homosexuality and the Lockstep—Kangaroo Courts—Disgraceful West Virginia —Wheeling—Clarksburg's Two Meals a Day—The "Utter Detachment of the Judiciary"—Grafton Another of the Worst Three—Water and Filth for Floor Covering— Parkersburg, Fairmont and Huntington—A Comparison —Corrupting the Young—Spreading Venereal Disease— St. Augustine—What the Visitor Does Not See—High Tide at the Tampa Jail—A Case of Total Lack and Utter Indifference—Jacksonville, a Crucible of Corruption —"Guaranteed Criminal: Made in American Jails"— Checking Disease Without, Promoting It Within—Obsolete Birmingham — A Public Scandal — Letting "Bad Enough" Alone — Indiana Jails — Indiana's Criminal Treatment of the Insane.

CHAPTER V.

TREATMENT OF WOMEN

The Factor of the Male Jailer—Unrestricted Looseness —Girls at Gainesville—Demoralizing the Adolescent— Mrs. O'Hare and the Missouri State Prison — Emma Goldman—Bathing Rules—The "Hole"—The So-called Hospital — Homo-sexuality — Whipping Women—Virginia State Penitentiary—Women as the Cause of Crime.

CHAPTER VI.

NARCOTICS

Parish Prison at New Orleans—The "Trusty" System —A Morphine Scandal—Creating Drug Addicts—Medically Sanctioned Traffic — Unspeakable Missouri — Eighteen Prisoners in Three Cells—Sick and Insane—A Hundred Years of Overcrowding—"We Sure Do Need One" —St. Louis and Kansas City—Smuggling Narcotics— Cocaine, Opium, Yenshee and Morphine—"Doing Your Bit on a Pill"—The Visitors' Screen—The Prison "Underground"—Detecting Drugs — Treatment of Drug Addicts.

CHAPTER VII.

"TAKING THE VINEGAR OUT OF 'EM"

Texas Jails: Galveston, Houston, Corpus Christi, Etc.
—Waco in a Class by Itself—Women's Quarters—Other
Bad Features—Arkansas: Fort Smith, Texarkana and
Berryville—New Hampshire—Oklahoma — Before State-
hood and Since—Giving Them the Benefit of the Doubt
— When and Why New Jails Are Built — Danville's
Dark Picture—Towels Unknown—Peoria's Grim Cru-
cible—Loathsome Conditions — Greenville's Miniature
Siberia—Prisoners' Complaints.

CHAPTER VIII.

THE HEART OF MARYLAND

Community Complacency — Maryland Penitentiary—
The "Blackjack King"—Official Complacency—Dissipat-
ing a Smoke Screen — A Curious Situation — When a
Crime Is Not a Crime—Dollars Versus Men—County
Jails—The Stone Vaults of Elkton—Chestertown's Wa-
tery Rat Hole—Three Men and a Boy—Centerville-
Easton: The Case of Fountain—Cambridge—Salisbury's
Sty—Baltimore City—Hagerstown's Iron Slats—Towson
—Westminster, a Neglected Tomb—The Result.

CHAPTER IX.

PERSONNEL—ESCAPES—ADMINISTRATION

Calibre of Officials—Lack of Equipment—Necessary
Qualifications—A Unique Situation—Sexual Perverts—
Mental Defectives—How the Crucible Shapes the Un-
formed Official—Escapes—A Leather Ladder and a File
—Fire-arms—"Prison Simples"—Wooden Guns—Prison
Table Etiquette—"Flying a Kite"—A Message in Cipher
—The Rule of Silence—The "Snitch" System—Some In-
genious Escapes—Contraband—Jailers and Wardens—A
School of Penology the Remedy—Courses of Study, Etc.

CHAPTER X.

YEARS OF HORROR

Nebraska Jails—Omaha's Swift Deterioration—A Subject for American Women—A Century and a Half at Charleston—How White Women Are Treated—Colored Women—Pest Holes of South Carolina — Twenty-eight Instances—"Wiggle Tails"—Michigan's Leadership—Detroit—Chicago Jail a Synonym for Everything Vicious—Demoralizing Idleness—From Richmond to the Border Strip.

CHAPTER XI.

SPECIFIC REMEDIES

Workshops of Crime—Dirt — Showers — Compulsory Bathing—Fumigation—Clothes — Eating in Cells—Overcrowding—Hygiene—Infectious Diseases—Syphilis—Tuberculosis — Prison Doctors — Drug Addicts — Narcotic Cures—Segregation of Juveniles, Sexes and Unconvicted —Unnecessary Delays—Exercise and Recreation—"Pampering" Prisoners—Reading Matter—"Kangaroo Courts" — Duty of the Judge — Fee System of Feeding — The Curse of Idleness—How It May Be Eliminated—"Judicial Districts"—Farming—Compulsory Work Law—State Jails — Prisoners' Compensation — Inspection — Federal Jails—Federal Responsibility.

CHAPTER XII.

ESTABLISHING A NEW ORDER

Treating the Criminal, Not the Crime—Weeding Out the Unfit—Curing Psychic Diseases—A "Receiving Prison"—Felony Cases—Misdemeanants—The Pure Indeterminate Sentence—The "Genuine" Criminal—Punishment No Deterrent—National Identification Bureau—How It Should Function—Bureau at Leavenworth—Some Deceptive Cases—Out of the Dark Ages.

CHAPTER I.

A HUMAN DUMPING GROUND

The True Definition of "JAIL"—Difference Between a Jail and a Prison—"A Debauch of Dirt, Disease and Degeneracy"—The Untried—The Unconvicted—To Diminish Crime and the Number of Criminals—The Innocent—What the Public Does Not Know—The Increasing Danger.

If I were asked to give a definition of the word "JAIL," I think the following would be about as accurate as I could possibly make it:

JAIL: An unbelievably filthy institution in which are confined men and women serving sentence for misdemeanors and crimes, and *men and women not under sentence who are simply awaiting trial.* With few exceptions, having no segregation of the unconvicted from the convicted, the well from the diseased, the youngest and most impressionable from the most degraded and hardened. Usually swarming with bedbugs, roaches, lice, and other vermin; has an odor of disinfectant

13

and filth which is appalling; supports in complete idleness countless thousands of able bodied men and women, and generally affords ample time and opportunity to assure inmates a complete course in every kind of viciousness and crime. A melting pot in which the worst elements of the raw material in the criminal world are brought forth blended and turned out in absolute perfection.

There is only one trouble with the above definition—it is not quite strong enough. For there are conditions so revolting that their discussion is not permissible. Exceptions exist, of course, both in our larger cities and our smaller towns, but based upon an experience of many years as the only Inspector of Prisons of the United States Government, I believe I can conservatively say that the above definition will apply to fully eighty-five per cent. of the jails throughout the country. The exceptions are so few and far between that they stand out like a clean patch of snow in a street of swirling mud. They but serve to increase the wonder that nearby communities, at least, do not take a lesson from them, instead of permitting their own institutions to degenerate year by year into increasingly repellent human dumping grounds.

Remember, when I say "jails" I do not mean "prisons." In the pure sense, there is a difference, and a vast difference, between these two types of institutions. Men and women are confined in *prison,* strictly speaking, after they have been convicted of an offense of a grave character which involves moral turpitude. They are confined in jail after they have been convicted of misdemeanors, such as being drunk and disorderly, petit larceny, working on Sunday, etc. Also (and here is the great difference) jails are used for the confinement of men and women who have been arrested *charged* with committing crimes or misdemeanors, but who have not yet been tried.

15

As a general rule, persons are sentenced to jail for comparatively short periods of from thirty days to a year. They are sentenced to prison for periods of from one year to life.

Although there is a clean-cut difference between a jail and a prison or penitentiary as institutions, it is true that the word *prison* has come to be used in a general sense, denoting any place where people are confined for punishment or while awaiting trial. Penitentiaries (or prisons) and penitentiary inmates will be touched on in this book as circumstances warrant, but I intend to deal mainly with the jails of the country because every person charged with misdemeanors or crimes, whether man, woman or child, goes to jail before being sent to any other institution, be it a reform school, reformatory, house of correction or penitentiary. It is in a sense a preparatory school of crime, where the more or less raw material is first molded into shape. If the great multitude of criminals and the amount of crime are to be reduced, the jails of the country must be altered. At present they are initial breeding places of corruption. Nine chances out of ten when a prisoner leaves them for the reformatory or prison, the "job" is done.

And if, in reading this book, you should attempt to ease your conscience by the thought, either spoken or unspoken, that after all men and women should not get into jail, and they would not be compelled to undergo such treatment, NEVER LOSE SIGHT OF THE FACT THAT MANY OF THEM ARE INNOCENT AND ARE EVENTUALLY LEGALLY DECLARED SO. BUT NEVERTHELESS, THESE PERSONS SIMPLY AWAITING TRIAL RECEIVE, IN NINETY-FIVE PERCENT. OF THE JAILS OF THE COUNTRY, EXACTLY THE SAME TREATMENT AS THOSE SERVING SENTENCE.

17

Nor is the percentage of innocent persons negligible. Take a typical year in New York City. Of 3,148 cases disposed of by the District Attorney's office, in which the guilt or innocence of the defendant was directly in question, 332 were acquitted. In other words, about one out of every ten persons was found to be innocent.

During the past sixteen years I have visited approximately 1,500 jails in the United States, many of them over and over again, from Boston to San Francisco, and from Brownsville, Texas, to Seattle, Washington; as well as Porto Rico and Alaska, in addition to a very large number of prisons, reformatories, reform schools, houses of correction and asylums for the criminal insane. I have, I suppose, talked to forty or fifty thousand prisoners of every age and description, and of every degree of criminality, degradation and viciousness; listened to their stories; investigated every phase of the conditions under which they live, and employed them in various capacities.

So my conclusions are not of the parlor variety. I do not think convicted men and women are mistreated angels in disguise, nor do I believe they should winter in Palm Beach and summer in Newport. On the contrary, I believe that a large percentage of those convicted are confirmed criminals who, when their criminal tendencies are definitely ascertained, should be culled out, classified as incurable and placed in confinement for the balance of their lives. It can readily be seen, therefore, that in any consideration of plans to diminish crime and the number of criminals there are two principal matters to be accomplished: (1) the prevention of any conditions which tend to create, encourage or develop criminals; and (2) the proper classification and treatment of offenders including the permanent confinement of those who are shown to be incurable.

Concerning the widely prevailing view

19

that many innocent persons are convicted of crime, I do not believe this is borne out by the facts. Under the law, every presumption is in favor of those charged with crime, and it is only in exceptionally rare cases that the innocent are convicted, although thousands are charged with crime, of course, who are subsequently acquitted. However, I do most decidedly believe that even those convicted, to say nothing of the unconvicted, should be treated at least like human beings—and allowed at any rate the common decencies which are given to ordinary animals. But from my knowledge of general standards of living compared with institutional standards, and of institutional standards compared with jails, *I declare that a jail is a debauch of dirt, disease and degeneracy.*

What the public does not know is that when the judge says "Thirty days in jail," he is sentencing the prisoner to many more things than mere confinement in an institution. If the facts were

20

known, in most instances the sentence would actually read:

"I not only sentence you to confinement for thirty days in a bare, narrow cell in a gloomy building, during which time you will be deprived of your family, friends, occupation, earning power, and all other human liberties and privileges; but in addition I sentence you to wallow in a putrid mire demoralizing to body, mind and soul, where every rule of civilization is violated, where you are given every opportunity to deteriorate, but none to improve, and where your tendency to wrong-doing cannot be corrected, but only aggravated."

The American jail itself is our most evil preventable condition. Others, such as current trial procedure, alteration of the parole system, a stricter regulation of bail, preventing the reproduction of the unfit, etc.,* while valuable in themselves, pale beside the lurid influence of the American jail. Lurid, not only because of the rank injustice to the criminal, but of the still ranker injustice to society. Such conditions do not correct the criminal; they do not punish from the social standpoint of preventing repetition; but instead they defeat the very purpose of incarceration by creating and fostering criminal tendencies, desires and purposes to the utmost.

But I cannot believe that if the public knew of this situation, it would continue to tolerate such a state of affairs. For in spite of the fact that those connected with the jails are conversant with existing conditions, I do not think that the av-

---

*I purposely will not deal at all with economic causes of crime—poverty, unemployment, etc.—in this book as that would lead off into the realm of theory and discussions and must at all events be solved by evolution or drastic changes in social forms or both, while I find that right here now within our social order there are glaring causes of crime which are totally uncalled for and which are easily susceptible of removal. It is with these tangible obstacles and their practical destruction that I am concerned here.

erage citizen, callous and indifferent
though he usually is presumed to be,
would for one moment permit their con-
tinuance if the facts were fully brought
to his attention.

I do not mean to say that from time
to time in certain localities these barbarous conditions have not been brought to
light, but invariably after a few days of
excitement the community goes complacently on its way, while conditions are
permitted to remain as they were. This
has always struck me as an apparent
rather than a real community complacency; for while it is true that the jails
are public institutions and therefore
the charges of the public, of course the
public collectively does not run them,
but reposes this responsibility in selected
officials. So that, when a vicious public
condition is exposed, it naturally looks to
officials in charge to carry out promised
changes and permits the matter to rest
there. In at least ninety-five instances
out of a hundred, however, after the

23

transient excitement dies away, old conditions continue. I daresay that not one citizen in such a community ever inquires afterward whether the promised changes have been effected. The situation resolves itself into that old truism, "What is everybody's business is nobody's business"; but the fact is that the condition of the jail in any community is very much the business of the average citizen, not only for humane reasons, but as a matter of personal self-protection.

For the man in jail today is the man who will be out tomorrow. Many of him are just awaiting trial and are subsequently proven guiltless. Many, also, of the guilty ones would respond to humane and scientific treatment. If the treatment which they receive in jail, and the surroundings forced upon them are such as to turn them out with criminal tendencies which were lacking or dormant when they went in, you, Mr. Average Citizen, may be the one to suffer. It may be your safe blown open, your house burglarized, your wife or daughter attacked, your automobile that may be stolen, your family to which disease is spread. In any case, a jail system which constantly turns out more and worse criminals is daily increasing instead of diminishing these dangers. And I say that ninety-five percent. of the jails of America, however widely separated, are driving with uniform efficiency toward one great end—the making of hardened, vicious and abandoned criminals.

Public opinion can do more to place our jails generally on a rational level than the occasional attempts of officials here and there. I am, therefore, laying the following facts before and appealing to not only the individuals and bodies having direct authority to make changes, but to every citizen, in the hope that when he knows the conditions he will pass judgment and will demand swift execution of that judgment.

CHAPTER II.

CHARACTERISTIC CONDITIONS

Criminals are being made in our jails not by any conspiracy or conscious effort, but by an atrocious neglect and indifference. This is characteristic of every section of the country, although perhaps a little worse, if that be possible, in the south. It is true of the great State of New York, as well as of thinly populated Arizona; of the thriving city of Seattle, the gateway to Alaska, as well as of the most benighted feud counties of Kentucky. To show how universal these conditions are, I shall not consider the country in geographical order, but shall purposely jump from one section to another, ranging the west against the north, the north against the east, and so on.

Suppose we begin with New York. Here we find that, generally speaking the jails and jail system compare favorably with those in other states. Yet right in Albany within five minutes ride of the State Capitol is a vivid example of what I mean when I say that "the average jail is a debauch of dirt, disease and degeneracy."

Here are two institutions—the Albany County Penitentiary and the Albany County Jail—housed in one building and administered by one set of officials. Though named differently, they are both practically jails. In the so-called penitentiary, men and women are confined who have been sentenced to from three months to a year. In the jail are confined persons awaiting trial and persons sentenced to from five to fifteen days, the latter class being known among the jail officials as the "bum squad."

27

The institution was built in 1847,—just 76 years ago,—and the antiquated, uncivilized design of that day is still retained.

The cells are entirely without light, even of the artificial kind. When in some emergency the officials must have light in the cells, a candle is used. The cells are only eight feet long, and they are so dark that even in the day time, standing directly in front of the closed barred door, it is impossible to see to the rear of the cell. I had a photographer attempt to take a picture of the interior of one of these cells, but although he took a long time exposure, the best picture he could obtain showed only two feet into the cell.

All the cells are exactly alike. They each are eight feet long, four feet wide, and seven feet high, with a barred door two feet wide. Each contains a cot two feet wide, allowing but a two foot width for the prisoner to move in, and a bucket for toilet purposes which is cleaned, supposedly, every morning.

Now draw out on the floor of your home a space eight by four feet—the size of a small rug—imagine that over it is a ceiling seven feet high, that just half of the width of your space is given up to a cot, that in one corner stands a reeking bucket, and that out of this totally dark, evil-smelling space, with its enclosing walls, you cannot move for forty-three hours at a time.

For this is exactly what happens to the prisoners at the Albany County Penitentiary and Albany County Jail. Each saturday at noon they are locked in their cells, not to come out until monday morning at 7:30, except for a voluntary chapel attendance on sunday. During the remainder of the week they are similarly locked in about twelve hours of each day. In the 103 hours spent this way each week a prisoner can do absolutely nothing, can read absolutely nothing, and has for sole inspiration an odoriferous bucket, a most edifying companion and one indeed calculated to make him reflect on the error of his ways and lead him to a better life.

The odor throughout the entire jail would sicken an animal. The bedding is dirty beyond belief. The place is so full of vermin that the deputy, Mr. Fish, cautioned me not to brush against walls, pipes or anything else. The institution has no "delousing" facilities for newly-arrived prisoners, and Mr. Fish frankly admitted his helplessness in combatting this plague.

How does the "long term" man in the so-called penitentiary spend the remaining 65 hours in the week when he is not locked in his cell? Is he learning to become a worth while citizen, to improve his hands and mind, to correct at all his evil tendencies? Judge for yourself.

There is only work enough here for about half of them. The remainder leave their cells at 7:30, have breakfast, and then spend the rest of the day in a large room under the eyes of a guard on sit in utter and complete idleness, or, if an elevated platform. Here they just they so desire, play cards and other games of chance. There are no books or magazines for these prisoners, the "library" (consisting of agricultural reports, sermons and a few other volumes) being for the use of the hospital prisoners only. As the story about the farm boy goes, during the week they "set and think" and on Sunday they "just set."

If a man is serving a sentence of a year, he spends 5,536 hours in the dark, cramped, slimy, smelly, vermin-infested cell previously described, and 3,380 hours sitting on a bench doing absolutely nothing, or engaged in such delectable methods of whiling away the time as playing cards, and telling or listening to filthy stories and tales of crime. He gets no fresh air, no exercise, no recreation. After spending a year in such fashion, he is of course well equipped in every way to go out and earn an honest living. If he does not, naturally he has no one to blame but himself, so will have to be cured by being sent back for another year for further mental and physical discipline.

There is a hospital provided for sick prisoners—but what a hospital! There is an ancient, broken-down, rusty stove with pots and dishes to match, which are the only facilities for preparing the food which the sick require, and an utter lack of cleanliness and sanitation. Even here the sheets are black with all kinds of grime, and liberally sprinkled with bread crumbs and other particles of food. The odor, if anything, is a little worse than in the rest of the institution.

The short termers and men awaiting trial occupy a separate section in the part of the institution called the jail. These men live in complete idleness, spending their time playing cards, smoking and talking, in "idle parlors" made by barring off the space in front of their respective cell blocks. Some of the men awaiting trial at the time of my last visit

had already been in from five or six
weeks to three months. The conditions
in these quarters are exactly the same in
all details as those in the so-called penitentiary.

The same is true of the women's building, with the exception that it is perhaps
a trifle cleaner.

The institution generally is not only
antiquated, but decayed. It is actually
falling to pieces. The walls are crum-
bling, the roof leaks in a dozen places, the
boilers are falling apart from age, and
the pipes are rotting and choked with
rust. In one place the wall bulges in a
manner that looks decidedly unsafe.

My last visit to the Albany County
Penitentiary and Jail was about the middle of January, 1922. Mr. Fish, the
deputy, who had been in office only since
the first of the year, was so thoroughly
revolted at the conditions under which
these men were living that he simply
"boiled over." He bitterly condemned
the existence of such conditions, and

made the significant statement that he had lived in Albany all his life, had passed the jail hundreds of times, and had never had the slightest idea that such was the state of affairs. I call this statement significant because it tallies with the situation revealed in hundreds of communities where I have made investigations. I have found this lack of knowledge to exist not only in the citizens of the community, but many times indeed in governing boards and authorities even after they had been connected with or in charge of penal institutions for some time.

At Blackwell's Island, or Welfare Island as it is now called, in the institution for men the cell block is in very bad shape. The cells are dirty and emit a foul odor, the abominable "night bucket" system being in vogue here also. In fact, cells, bunks, bedding and everything in the cell house are unspeakably vile.

The institution is so thoroughly infested with vermin that, I was informed

34

by one of the officers, the authorities have contracted with a company of "exterminating engineers"in New York to come over once every week to endeavor to keep at a minimum the thousands of new and unwelcome visitors who multiply during each interval.

The cells are about the same size as those at Albany, although my recollection is that the doors here are only about eighteen inches instead of two feet wide. Here the prisoners have an hour of grace Saturday afternoon, compared to Albany. They are locked in their cells at one o'clock instead of noon and get out a little earlier Monday morning, so that they have only 95 hours a week to spend in these damp, clammy, shallow, vermin-infested caverns.

In justice to the institution, I wish to say that some of the departments are fairly clean and well kept, but the cell houses are so old I do not believe they can ever be entirely freed of vermin unless the place is hermetically sealed and fumigated. But even if this were done, the officials are maintaining the cell houses in such a filthy condition that it would be but a short time until they were again housing myriads of vermin. The general appearance of the cell houses shows that little if any real effort is being made to keep them clean.

Although we are concerned here mainly with jails, one cannot discuss penal matters in New York State without taking cognizance of its most celebrated penal institution, which has of late years occupied so much space in the press—Sing Sing.

In general construction and in equipment for the housing of the prisoners Sing Sing Prison is worse even than the jails at Albany and at Blackwell's Island. The cell house was built in 1824, just ninety-nine years ago. The cells are similar to those of Blackwells and Albany, except that here only one-half the door is barred, allowing of course only half of that meagre foot or two or gloom which penetrates the cells at Blackwells and Albany. When I was last there, in the latter part of January, 1922, the cell house was freezing cold. You could "see your breath" when you talked. I was very uncomfortable, even with my overcoat on. It is just as though the men are living in little stalls of damp stone housed in a large, unheated barn. As a matter of fact, I have seen some prison barns which I should infinitely prefer as living quarters.

It is true that a new cell house has been begun, which will be finished in two or three years, but this does not mitigate the fact that the present building should have been scrapped at least a half century ago. Indeed, if the keepers of old Newgate Prison in England—that symbol of prison horrors—could have seen this cell house even as far back as fifty years ago, they would have admitted that, to use a colloquialism, old Newgate "had nothing on" Sing Sing. To my mind, it is and has been for generations a monstrous outrage to confine human beings in this cell house, no matter what their degree of moral turpitude.

From Ossining let's jump to Cleveland, on the Great Lakes. Here in the very heart of the city, practically on the square, and almost directly opposite the new and beautiful Cleveland Hotel, stands the jail. In appearance from the outside it resembles an old-fashioned church. On the inside its appearance is anything but churchly. It is a crying disgrace and a festering sore—a whited sepulchre in the very midst of this respectable community. The tentacles of disease nursed and propagated here have spread undoubtedly into many a Cleveland home. The place is so old and so saturated with the effluvia of foulness, so poorly lighted and so frightfully ventilated, that it is a matter of practical impossibility to keep it clean. It has, if anything, more than the usual quota of bed bugs and "cooties," and it pollutes the air with a combination odor of disinfectant and worse that is simply over-powering.

Some idea of the intensity of its smell may be gained from the fact that they spend approximately $1,200.00 a year for insecticide to give the tormented prisoners some relief from the burden of vermin, so I was informed by one of the jailers upon my last visit there, a comparatively short time ago. Even in these days of inflated prices, the sum of $1,200.00 will pay for an enormous amount of insecticide. The odor of a comparatively small quantity of it, where a jail is so poorly ventilated as this one, is by no means pleasant. Try and imagine the sickening effect when a jail is literally saturated with it from cellar to roof.

For many long years this unbelievably vile place has been complacently used to house men and women, many of whom after spending weeks in this intolerable hole, were never even convicted of crime. And even though the money for a new jail was appropriated several years ago, the actual construction, begun but recently, has already been abandoned.

Right here are illustrated some of the difficulties under which the Federal Government labors in its efforts to secure suitable quarters for its thousands of prisoners. The Federal Government has three large penitentiaries for men but no jails of its own. Instead, it boards its jail prisoners at so much per day in the various city and county jails throughout the country. Where conditions are objectionable the Government sometimes transfers these prisoners to other jails, but in the larger cities it must use the jails, be they good, bad or indifferent, at least during terms of Federal Court, when prisoners awaiting trial must be immediately available. One investigation which I made of the Cleveland Jail was upon the suggestion of United States District Judge Westerhaver, at Cleveland, and I discussed the conditions with him. But, much as he and the Department of Justice would have liked to improve them, there was absolutely nothing they could do for the Federal prisoners, as it was impracticable to remove them to a greater distance.

From the Great Lakes let us go to the great southwest, where we are so often told that the milk of human kindness flows in greater abundance, and where there is supposed to be a more sympathetic understanding and toleration of the other fellow's faults. One would naturally suppose that here, of all places, efforts would be made to give the prisoner a fairly human habitation, facilities for keeping himself clean, and an opportunity to preserve his self-respect, if he has any self-respect within him. Well, to state the matter briefly, in the majority of the places of Arizona, he gets no such facilities and no such opportunities. If anything, he gets worse treatment on the average than elsewhere.

Phoenix, the county seat of Maricopa County, is the largest city in Arizona.

The jail here consists of a dirty, dilapidated, two-story structure in the rear of the court house. The court house itself is not any too well kept, but alongside the jail it seems a model of cleanliness. The jail consists of two tiers or "ranges" of cells facing a common corridor. Two hammocks are swung in each cell. The hammocks are never cleaned, as I have visited this jail on seven or eight occasions and have always found them covered with filth. The jail crawls with vermin. And although it is only supposed to accommodate about forty prisoners, there have been occasions when from seventy-five to one hundred Federal prisoners, to say nothing of a considerable number of State prisoners, were packed in this foul cage. At such times the intense heat in this section of the country, added to the usual condition of the institution, combined to produce such an odor as can neither be imagined nor described. Four or five hammocks are then swung in one cell, which otherwise uncomfortably accommodates two. By packing the prisoners in the cells as closely as they can be packed there is not sufficient room. Many of the prisoners sleep on top of the cell block,, lying helter-skelter on the hard steel.

As in the great majority of jails throughout the United States no effort whatever is made to separate the sick from the well. When it is considered that a very large percentage of prisoners is suffering from venereal disease, many of the cases being in an infectious stage, that they use common drinking cups, sleep on unwashed bedding used possibly by a hundred other prisoners, both sick and well, have common toilet facilities, lack a proper amount of cubic air space, and are by virtue of this overcrowding thrown in the closest possible contact, the amount of disease which is thus communicated must be staggering.

The average number of tuberculosis cases in Arizona is considerably greater than in practically any state in the Union,

43

due to the fact that so many patients go there to be cured. A considerable percentage of those in jail is suffering with tuberculosis. But as with other diseased prisoners, no attempt whatever is made to segregate them from the healthy and here, living in filth, with little fresh air and much overcrowding, they exist amid conditions which are ideal not only for the quick progress of the disease in themselves, but also, which is far worse, for spreading it to others who had up until then escaped it. In fact, the Phoenix jail is typical of the fact that, of all public institutions, jails alone seem to be immune from any considerations of hygiene.

In nearly every state there are two cities which are rivals. Phoenix is much the largest city in Arizona, but if Tucson is not in reality a rival, she thinks she is. Whatever Phoenix does, Tuscon tries to go her just one better. She succeeds notoriously in the matter of jails. Here also the building is a small two story affair back of the courthouse and is a second Phoenix with the colors painted a little darker. At times it is frightfully overcrowded. And to get some idea of what that means one only needs to know that the temperature here on occasions runs anywhere from one hundred and five to one hundred and ten degrees in the shade.

Within the past year or two Prescott has built a new jail. Prescott is the only place in Arizona I have seen of which it could be said that the jail was always kept in a clean condition. It is a very much smaller place than either Tucson or Phoenix, but it sets an example that these two would do well to follow, except in one respect. For here there are also the same conditions of overcrowding. Anywhere from fifty to seventy-five prisoners are confined at times where only about thirty or thirty-five can be accommodated decently.

At Globe, the county seat of Gila County, and the heart of the copper

45

country of the United States, the jailer frankly admitted that the bedding was never washed, it being found easiest and most convenient (for the jailer of course) to use it until it fell apart from wear and filth.

At Florence, on the occasion of my last visit, the jailer was a Mexican who appeared at ease only in muck. The place was indescribably nasty.

At Nogales, the floor of the jail was littered several inches deep with scraps of food and filth and trash of all descriptions, while the prisoners were thrown in helter-skelter, young and old, convicted and unconvicted, diseased and healthy. The jail is in the heart of the town, practically on the main street, and I have no doubt but that every adult in the town passes it twenty-five or thirty times a year. Yet I will venture the statement that not one citizen in Nogales out of one hundred has ever been inside the jail on a visit of inspection, or has the remotest idea of what the conditions really are. Almost the same can be said of the other communities in Arizona which I have mentioned. This must indeed be true, because as I have said before, I cannot believe that if the average citizen were aware of these conditions, he would tolerate them for an instant.

CHAPTER III.

"NO BUSINESS OF MINE"

Kansas, the "Model" State—Kansas City's filthy little Dungeon—Wichita, One of the Worst in the Country—A Revolving Cell House—Overcrowding, Rats, Bugs, Etc.—Unhealthy, Uncomfortable and Indecent—"Against the Government"—A Typical Jailer—Other Kansas Jails—Kansas State Penitentiary — Good-hearted "Smoky" Allen—A Jail De Luxe—Supernatural Sight—A Comic Opera Inspiration—Private Citizens and Public Prisoners in Seattle—The Case of Phillips—How American Communities View Their Jails—What Happens to Those Who Reveal Rotten Conditions—The Jails of Pennsylvania—A Sink of Iniquity—A Coop Without a Yard—Media—Philadelphia—Camden, Frightful and Typical—Pittsburg — Pennsylvania's Smaller Jails — The Vicious Fee System—Exploiting the Prisoners—An Easy Way to Get Rich.

Now let us climb aboard the Santa Fe and see what Kansas does for its prisoners. Surely here must be a model for the rest of the country. For isn't Kansas in the very vanguard of civilization? Wasn't it Kansas that took the lead in abolishing liquor, and the deadly cigarette and the still more deadly public drinking cup; Kansas that produced

48

Henry Allen and William Allen White, who have written such inspiring articles in answer to the query, "What's the matter with Kansas?"

Regardless of how she is "bleeding" with prosperity in other directions, when it comes to the matter of the treatment of her prisoners in jail, she is really bleeding at every pore from the same neglect, indifference and brutality as the majority of the other states in the Union.

The jail at Kansas City, Kansas, the largest city in the state, is a filthy little dungeon unfit for human habitation. And I have always regarded the county jail at Wichita as one of the three worst I have ever seen, the two others being located in Charleston, South Carolina, and Grafton, West Virginia.

The jail at Wichita is extremely old and is of a design which was obsolete twenty years ago. As far as I can recall at the moment there are only two or three other jails of similar design in the United States. Each cell is practically triangular in shape. The cells are placed in a revolving cylinder which is turned with a lever. When a prisoner is admitted he goes up a runway into a cell. By revolving the entire cylinder practically all cells are turned toward a wall, the idea apparently being to increase the difficulty of escape. A prisoner may go to bed at night with his cell door facing the east and wake up with it facing the west, if the cylinder was turned during the night to admit a new prisoner. The human refuse was carried into a trough at the base of the cylinder, where it was sometimes allowed to remain as long as a week at a time. The protests of the prisoners became so bitter and insistent that the jailers were forced to take cognizance of them, so the use of these triangular horrors was finally abandoned and the prisoners permitted to occupy cots in every nook and corner of the jail where there was sufficient room to place one.

The jail accommodated about twelve

prisoners. But there were thirty-one Federal prisoners alone in confinement on one of my visits to this institution, twenty-eight of them Industrial Workers of the World, I. W. W. or "Wobblies," as they have come to be known, and the other three "bootleggers," to say nothing of several state prisoners. These thirty-one men, crowded into a room designed to hold twelve, had for shelter a roof which leaked in a dozen places and supplied the floor with unhealthy little pools of water. The jail was inadequately heated and the prisoners suffered frightfully when the weather was cold.

Dirt reigned supreme. The bedding was never washed. Some of the blankets were entirely black, so that it was impossible to tell what their original color had actually been. There were bed bugs by the thousands. I took one of the cots, placed it in the bath tub and turned on the water. This is an old trick used by prisoners to relieve themselves in a measure from these pests. The moment the water started to run the bugs started to leave, and I believe an actual count would have disclosed that at least three hundred deserted this one cot, so that when I say there were thousands of them in the jail, I actually mean thousands, and do not intend it as hyperbole or as a figure of speech in any sense.

The place swarmed with rats of the large sewer variety, which ran across the prisoners' faces as they slept and generally tormented them almost beyond endurance. The prisoners would set traps and catch as many as six or eight rats a night. The floor was littered with filth and rubbish of all kinds, with papers, remnants of decaying food, and every imaginable kind of trash, and from it all arose a stench that was positively nauseating.

I mentioned a bath tub, but do not confuse that with the attractive white affair in your own home. The Wichita bath tub was covered with a crust of dirt and grime a quarter of an inch thick.

Certainly no person with a single ounce of self-respect would care to use it. I do not believe there is an animal in any zoo or menagerie in the United States, assuming him to have any intelligence at all, who would trade his quarters for those of this jail. Here the prisoners have only what is unhealthy, uncomfortable and indecent; and of this they have every variety. One of the prisoners said to me: "Before God, Mr. Fishman, if a man was not against the Government when he went in, he surely would be before he got out."

You will agree it is not so difficult to understand this state of mind under such conditions. Indeed, such conditions, as I contend, do not correct the criminal, but serve to aggravate his criminal tendencies.

Both the sheriff and the jailer freely admitted that the jail was filthy from top to bottom, making this statement in about the same casual way as they would have commented upon the weather.

They did not seem to feel any responsibility whatsoever for its condition, nor that they were called upon to remedy it. They took it quite as a matter of course. However, they did not differ in these respects from hundreds of other jail officials throughout the United States with whom I have talked. It is typical of the attitude which I find to exist practically everywhere among officials in jails when the living conditions or general welfare of the prisoners in their custody are discussed.

I recommended to the Department that the federal prisoners be removed immediately and that the conditions existing in this institution be called to the attention of the Governor of Kansas in order that he might use his power to obtain their correction. The federal prisoners were taken to different jails, some of them going to the one at Topeka, which is far from being a model institution, but yet is infinitely superior to the one at Wichita. Subsequently they were transferred to the jail at Leavenworth, where the conditions have been somewhat improved in recent years so that the jail there is at least in a fairly habitable condition.

With very few exceptions, the other jails in Kansas are only slightly better than the one at Wichita.

While as a general rule the conditions in prisons are far better than in jails, some of them being splendidly built institutions very efficiently administered, the Kansas State Penitentiary is not by any means so far advanced as many of the other prisons in the United States. It is extremely old and out of date, the cell houses being very dark and the cells in which the prisoners are confined being very poorly lighted and ventilated.

The "no business of mine" attitude on the part of jailers to which I have referred is often carried to an amusing length, and my mind goes back to an hilarious day that I spent in Jackson, Kentucky. Jackson, be it said, is the county seat of "Bloody Breathitt," the darkest and bloodiest of all the dark and bloody feud counties of this State. Jackson is located in one of the most inaccessible parts of Kentucky which is so hilly that I do not believe there is a single automobile in the entire county, one of the chief methods of locomotion being by mule or horseback. The jailer at this place was named Allen, and was called "Smoky" by the prisoners. "Smoky" was just so good hearted and indifferent that he not only did not care what the prisoners did inside the jail, but he also had no concern whatever with what they did on the outside. Any man who wanted to leave for three or four days to visit his family was cheerfully granted that permission, and if some of them failed to come back, as several did, why it was just too bad that some men had such poor memories. If a prisoner wanted to go across the river, half a mile away, he was allowed to go. It actually happened that prisoners who were supposed to be serving sentences became full of moonshine and fight and were placed under arrest by the town police, so that, technically speaking at least, they were placed in jail while they were in jail.

I protested to "Smoky," while standing in the jail yard with him, about allowing prisoners outside the jail. He replied that "there was a deputy with a gun who watched them." At the time there were several prisoners standing around listening to us talk. Upon being asked where this deputy was, "Smoky" said that he was *on the other side of the jail*. I explained to "Smoky" as tactfully as possible, that while I had always understood that these "hill billies" developed exceptionally good eyesight, I did not believe it was sufficiently keen to permit them to see through three of four stone walls and around corners. Smoky's only reply was, "Wal, he watches 'em all right," accompanying this statement by liberally spraying the grass with good old Kentucky tobacco juice.

While we were talking a "prisoner" walked up to us and said, "Lemme have the key, Smoky," which Smoky obligingly did. In a very matter of fact way the prisoner walked over to the jail, unlocked the door, let himself in, locked it after him, and in a few minutes appeared at the window and threw the key down to Smoky, who unconcernedly picked it up as though nothing whatever unusual had happened. I once saw a miniature comic opera in which a jail was so luxuriously conducted that the prisoners bitterly protested when their terms were up and the unfeeling jailer forced them to depart. I do not know who wrote this sketch, but have no doubt that he received his inspiration by watching the "goings on" at the Jackson jail.

The government moved the federal prisoners to Winchester, but I have no doubt that the state prisoners at Jackson are still enjoying all the comforts of home and that there is more than one tear shed at the expiration of their terms.

"Smoky" Allen was not the only hail-fellow-well-met in the jail world who couldn't differentiate between private citizens and public prisoners. He had his counterpart in a famous sheriff at Seattle. Whether a prisoner was a vicious cutthroat or merely a petty thief made no difference so long as he "stood in" with this official. Regardless of the danger and injustice to the community, such a prisoner who happened to have a "stand in" was allowed to roam around the city at will. If he was so fortunate as to own an automobile he could even take nice little trips into the country.

In my investigation I found that a prisoner by the name of Phillips, who was serving a sentence for white slavery, was being allowed to roam around the city almost daily. On one of these excursions I had him picked up and taken to the United States Marshal's office. It just happened that at the very moment I found this "prisoner" he was cursing his wife and threatening to "beat her up."

After I saw him safely stowed in the Marshal's office I went to the jail and asked to see Phillips. The deputy sheriff who was in at the time took me back in the jail and said to a prisoner who appeared to be allowed the run of the place, "Phillips, here's a federal inspector who wants to see you," at the same time winking "loudly" to "Phillips." The latter stuttered and stammered, but finally recovered himself and answered two or three questions as to how he was being treated which I had improvised for the occasion. When he got through I announced that Phillips was up in the Marshal's office, and the deputy jumped as though he had been shot.

Here, as in Jackson, Kentucky, was a situation in which extreme laxity in the handling of prisoners was as harmful to the community as extreme severity. Here you have a white slaver tried and convicted who as far as the community knows is safely stowed in jail, but who actually is prowling around in their midst; and, as I have said before, he was only one of many.

One would think that, when such a situation was made known, the local press would voice its condemnation and indignantly demand a change. But here a peculiar tendency of many American municipalities asserted itself with force. I refer to the tendency to maintain that whatever is, is as it should be in the particular city or town in question. And this brings us to one of the main issues of this book—the seemingly complacent attitude of American communities toward their jails and the reason for it.

Often when the most revolting conditions in an institution are brought to light, one or more of the local newspapers, because of some political affiliation or other motive of self interest, tries in every possible way to turn off the spotlight of public interest and to deaden public apprehension. To achieve this the paper or papers in question always resort to the simple expedient of minimizing the importance of the situation, to sneers and flat denials all along the line. If this does not accomplish their purpose they then attempt to distract attention from the real issue at stake by making a personal attack on the one who calls attention to existing evils. He is held up to the public ridicule and scorn as a fault finder or scoundrel who had some ulterior purpose of his own to serve. In some cases these attacks reach a pitch of venomous intensity that is astounding. Of course, it is not usual for all the newspapers in one community to take this attitude. Generally a portion of the local press can always be depended upon to fight for the public welfare. But the influence of this part of the press is often counteracted by the antagonistic journals, eager to lull the public into their previous inertia, because it is a well known weakness of human nature to be more interested in and give credence to sensational villifications of one individual than to deplorable general or institutional conditions, and because human nature loves the line of least resistance. For as H. L. Mencken has put it, "the public would rather believe a soothing fiction than a harsh fact." So, after the real issues have been beclouded by a smoke screen of personal accusation and inuendo, and the public has been confused and befooled, is it strange that institutional exposures often result only in a continued community complacency?

A newspaper situation such as outlined above made itself manifest in Seattle. Both the Post-Intelligencer and the Times made determined efforts, editorially and otherwise, to have this practice of the sheriff stopped. But the Seattle Star scouted the idea that there could be anything wrong at the jail and attempted to ridicule my findings out of existence. But when they failed to supress the matter in this way they began to publish article after article attacking me personally. They advanced such arguments in defence of the jail's illegal and immoral comic opera administration as calling me "a schoolboy from Washington," and of course accusing me of "playing in with certain newspapers and politicians who hate the sheriff for mere political reasons."

They devoted the entire front page of one issue to informing me of the community's attitude on the jail situation by stating that "the people resent your pernicious activity here," and advising me "YOU'D BETTER GET OUT" in big bold caps.

And all this in the face of the fact that the jail was nothing more than a dirty, gloomy cave. In one portion of the jail it is so dark that even in the middle of the brightest day there is not even sufficient light to read by. In fact, it is totally unfit, but all they have done about it so far is to "contemplate building a new one."

Let us continue our random flight. The jails of Pennsylvania with few exceptions are very old, and while perhaps a little better on the average than in many states are still far from being suitable for habitation by human beings. They are dungeons almost without exception, with cages for cells, practically all having little if any work for the prisoners, and the majority of them giving the prisoners no fresh air whatsoever, and little if any exercise. The one at York is unusually bad. It is a foul sink of iniquity, the food very poor, no work for the prisoners, no fresh air, little exercise, and generally unfit in every way. The jail at Harrisburg, the State capital, is just about as bad.

The jail at Erie had been described as "a large coop without a yard," which is a fitting designation. The last time I was there the overpowering odor of disinfectant told its own story. The jail at Media is clean and well kept, but entirely out of date. They "contemplate building a new one." They need more than "contemplating." Media is better,

65

however, than most of the others in that efforts are made to give the prisoners employment.

The jail at Philadelphia, known as the Moyamensing Prison, although very old, is well kept.

And while so close, we must turn our attention to its neighbor, Camden, New Jersey, just a ferry ride across the river. The jail at Camden is frightful—but a typical example of the average American jail. There is not the slightest effort to keep the place clean or separate the untried from the convicted. The bugs run riot. At the time I last visited this institution there were several rather high class young men confined there. One of them told me that his suffering from the vermin and filth was simply indescribable. The prisoners get no fresh air whatever and no exercise. No bathing rules are enforced, and the prisoners are as dirty a lot as ever I have seen. This is not their fault. A prisoner could not keep himself clean here if he tried.

As might be supposed, the keepers are the usual type of such officials, and the personnel is anything but an attractive one.

The jail at Pittsburgh is exceptionally good, as far as its physical features are concerned, but both here and at Philadelphia the same idleness prevails as generally throughout the country. The warden at Pittsburgh is very competent. He understands his duties thoroughly and personally sees to it that his orders are obeyed. He has been here over twenty years, which no doubt accounts in a measure for its efficient administration, since the institution reaps the benefit of his experience. It is entirely different at other places, where a jailer invariably changes with a change of administration. In this way, the jails are continually undergoing a new and "green" management. It would be well if most of the other jails in Pennsylvania and in other communities, such as Cleveland, would take a lesson from the jail at Pittsburgh.

Most of the smaller jails in the State

are just about on a par. They are very old, the majority of them with chinks instead of windows, and are as a rule, dark, gloomy and forbidding. Many still use the loathesome night buckets while others which have plumbing allow it to remain in a very leaky condition. Few of them give the prisoners any air, exercise or employment in any way. Mauch Chunk, Meadville, Carlisle, McConnellsburg, Indiana and Mifflintown, Gettysburg, Kittaning, Bedford—there is little, if any choice. And Newcastle, Lebanon and Williamsport are about the same, as are Milford, Towanda, Hollidaysburg, Montrose and Franklin.

But the worst feature of all in Pennsylvania is the fee system of compensating jailers. Instead of paying them a salary, many of the jailers are given a certain sum a day to feed the prisoners in their charge, the jailer retaining as part of his compenstation such portion of his allowance as is not paid out in food for the prisoners. For instance, if a jailer receives 50 cents per day per prisoner, and has a daily average of 50 prisoners in his jail, he will get $25.00 to pay for food. Every cent which he does not pay out for food goes into his own pocket. A more vicious system it would be impossible to conceive; that of one man lining his pockets in the same degree as he may withhold food from another.

Pennsylvania is not the only State in the Union which has the fee system of compensating jailers. There are many others, including Kentucky, Georgia, North Carolina, Virginia, Rhode Island, Missouri, Iowa, Minnesota, Tennessee, Arkansas, Ohio, Indiana and Florida. It is uniformly vicious wherever it is in vogue. I know of some places in the country where jailers or sheriffs have made as high as fifteen and twenty thousand dollars a year from the feeding of prisoners—or non-feeding, whatever you wish to call it.

In one place the sheriff was given 75 cents per day for feeding each prisoner in the jail. The number of prisoners averaged daily from seventy-five to one hundred. The sheriff made arrangements with a Chinaman who ran a small, cheap eating place in the town to feed the prisoners. The Chinaman used his own discretion. From the appearance of the prisoners' food, it did not seem as though anything that was left over in the Chinese place was now going to waste. He managed to furnish the prisoners two meals a day and make a profit at 13 cents. The sheriff thereby netted himself fifty to seventy-five dollars a day.

The prisoner naturally thinks he is being exploited, and in many cases he thinks correctly. He is thrown into jail in the most demoralizing surroundings, every incentive to cleanliness, decency, and self-respect is taken away from him, and then, as a crowning injury, his keeper is paid for feeding him in proportion to the amount of food he succeeds in forcing him to do without.

CHAPTER IV.

INSIDE THE CRUCIBLE.

Kentucky Jails—A "Black Hole of Calcutta"—Special Features of Bowling Green—Homo-sexuality and the Lockstep—Kangaroo Courts—Disgraceful West Virginia —-Wheeling—-Clarksburg's Two Meals a Day—-The "Utter Detachment of the Judiciary"—Grafton Another of the Worst Three—Water and Filth for Floor Covering —Parkersburg, Fairmont and Huntington—A Comparison —Corrupting the Young—Spreading Venereal Disease —St. Augustine—What the Visitor Does Not See—High Tide at the Tampa Jail—A Case of Total Lack and Utter Indifference—Jacksonville, a Crucible of Corruption—"Guaranteed Criminal; Made in American Jails"—Checking Disease Without; Promoting it Within—Obsolete Birmingham—A Public Scandal—Letting "Bad Enough" Alone—Indiana Jails—Indiana's Criminal Treatment of the Insane.

With the exception of the county institution at Louisville, and the county and city institutions at Covington, the jails of Kentucky are about on a par, which is to say that they are not fit to live in. The city jail at Louisville is another "Black Hole of Calcutta." It has not a single modern or up-to-date feature. The cells are narrow and dark and are equipped with canvas hammocks.

71

From one end of the jail to the other there is not one piece of bedding nor one bit of furniture. As to most of the other jails in the state, it is a difficult matter to tell which is the worst, London, Jackson, Paris, Georgetown, Owensboro, Pikeville, Barbourville, Catlettsburg, Frankfort, Paducah or Bowling Green, although the latter, at the time of my last visit had one distinctive feature which the others in this group lacked. Leaky plumbing had permitted a large quantity of matter from the toilets to accumulate on the floor, and this was tracked by the prisoners from one end of the jail to the other. Bowling Green also affords a typical illustration of the disease-breeding congestion existing in so many jails. Here sometimes as many as six prisoners are placed in a cell built to accommodate two. This necessitates stringing the hammocks so closely together that the men touch while sleeping, about as bad a practice as can possibly be imagined in institutions where

72

homo-sexuality is rampant. Some idea of how bad this practice really is may be gained by the reader when he knows that it was largely because of homo-sexuality that the barbarous lock-step had to be abandoned.

Do not lose sight of the fact that large numbers of these men have not been tried, and that many of them will be found to be innocent.

A notable feature of Kentucky jails is the prevalence of "kangaroo courts." A kangaroo court, for the benefit of the uninitiated, is an organization for maintaining discipline, which some jailers permit the prisoners to form among themselves. They make the rules and enforce them, and it must be said that in the majority of cases they do not temper justice with mercy. It is one way which some of the more indolent jailers have of "passing the buck," and thus relieving themselves of all responsibility for the discipline.

Where there is a fairly high class of

prisoners in jail, and the jailer indifferent, a kangaroo court may be of very distinct benefit, as the prisoners will make and enforce rules concerning cleanliness and sanitation, such as prohibiting throwing scraps of food on the floor, spitting, or other unclean habits. But in most cases the kangaroo court itself is composed of the lowest class of prisoners. In such jails the life of any prisoner who is not himself a member of the court is one of misery and persecution. The prisoners composing the court levy all kinds of ridiculous fines for imaginary offenses and carry out their edicts with brutality and callous indifference.

In the jail of Jackson, for instance, one of the prisoners with unusual courage refused to pay a fine which the kangaroo court imposed upon him. While he slept one of the members of the court placed a twisted piece of paper between his toes. Quietly he lit the end of it. With a shriek the prisoner awoke to find his foot aflame. This took place in the day time when the cells were opened and the prisoners allowed out in the corridor. And although it was witnessed by fellow prisoners, not one of them dared to protest or seek to save the offender from the wrath of the kangaroo court.

Conditions in the jails of the larger towns and cities in West Virginia are disgraceful. To make the round of them is to go through a monotonous repetition of filthy pest holes and breeding places of crime and disease. From Wheeling to Welch, and from Martinsburg to Huntington there is little if any choice. The jail of Wheeling runs itself, or did at the time of my last visit there, so far as any effort to keep it clean was concerned. There is the same old unwashed bedding, the usual army of vermin, the foul night buckets, and all the other inexcusable results of negligence and the general tendency to look upon a man as no longer entitled to be treated as a human being after he is once locked up, be he guilty or innocent.

The jail of Clarksburg was every bit as bad, while in addition there existed here another evil which is more or less common in a large number of other jails throughout the country. Two meals a day are fed. I do not criticise the feeding of two meals where men do no work, if they are nutritive and sufficient in quantity, with a proper interval of time between them. No such condition existed here. One meal was fed at seven A. M. and the other at twelve noon, nothing further being fed until seven o'clock the following morning. The prisoners therefore had two meals within a space of five hours, and not another bite to eat for a period of nineteen hours. Presumably it was more convenient for this jailer to feed at these times. Of course the fact that this method of feeding might not be sufficient and might possibly jeopardize the health of the prisoners was of no moment at all. They simply had no business to be locked up. But as if this were not enough, there was at the time of my last visit absolutely no variation in the food. Day after day, week after week, and month after month the first meal consisted of oatmeal and half a loaf of bread, and the second of beans and a half a loaf of bread. On Sunday a little meat was given the prisoners.

I had the Department at Washington discontinue the use of this, as well as several other jails in West Virginia, except during terms of holding Federal court. When the Department wrote to the United States district judge in the northern district of West Virginia, advising him of what I had found, and enclosing a copy of my report, that official replied that he "was very much surprised and shocked to learn from this report the condition of these jails, and the treatment of prisoners therein." It is a peculiar commentary upon the "utter detachment of the judiciary" and our judges' astounding lack of knowledge as to what becomes of a prisoner or how he is treated after sentence is pronounced. I have found a similar lack of knowledge to exist on numerous occasions. When I informed Federal Judge Evans at Louisville of the shocking conditions existing in the jail at Bowling Green he was simply swept off his feet with astonishment, and this, too, notwithstanding the fact that he had been sentencing prisoners there for many years. A judge cannot dispense justice until he knows what kind of an institution he is sending a man to, as a sentence of thirty days in one jail is often more punishment in reality than a sentence of six months in another institution. It is not by any means a rare thing for a prisoner to ask to have his sentence changed from six months in jail to one year in the penitentiary, if he happens to know the conditions existing in each. Any Federal judge in the United States could probably give many instances in which just such requests have been made of him.

I have heretofore mentioned that I consider the jail at Grafton one of the worst three that I have ever seen in the United States. It is in a very old and dilapidated building, while the basement in which the jail itself is located is unspeakably musty, damp and dirty. There are two large rooms, each equipped with a few cells, these rooms being located on opposite sides of a dungeon-like corridor, unclean and unpaved. At the time I was there the floor had not been cleaned for weeks and the place was gloomy and desolate beyond description. Due to leaky plumbing the entire floor was covered with dirty water and filth to the depth of one half inch to an inch. The prisoners were seated on boxes, with their feet on other boxes, this being the only method by which they could keep out of the water.

The jail at Philippi was a little better kept, although not by any means clean, while the one at Martinsburg, except that it had no water on the floor, was almost as bad as the one at Grafton. The floor was covered with papers, scraps of decayed food, and one or two dead rats.

Strange to say I found the jails at Parkersburg and Fairmont to be in good condition. This was so strange that, as one old jail-bird who had made the rounds of all of them informed me, these two places "stood out like a clean cut gem in a setting of phoney stones." The jail at Huntington was but in a fair condition. That at Charleston was dirty, the one at Princeton was dirtier, while the one at Bluefield outdid them both.

I visited the jail at Welch late at night, as I had but a comparatively short time to stay. The prisoners were all asleep. With a lantern the jailer took me down along the row of cells. In one cell into which he flashed his light I saw a prisoner of about forty-five years of age, whose face indicated that he had run the gamut of dissipation, actually occupying the same bunk or hammock with a boy who was not over fourteen years of age. What can one expect of prisoner possibilities when conditions such as this are allowed to exist?

At Princeton, West Virginia, I saw a prisoner with the worst case of syphilis that I have ever seen, and I have seen many hundreds of them in the penal institutions throughout the country. Part of his tongue was gone, and his mouth was literally half eaten away. Notwithstanding these facts, he was walking around in the inside corridor with all the other prisoners, using the same drinking glass, the same tub and the same toilet, and sleeping in a bed that had been used dozens of times before him and would be used dozens of times more by healthy prisoners after he left. The jailer knew no distinction; a prisoner was only a prisoner, and that was all there was to it. As at present conducted, this could well be the motto of the vast majority of jailers in the United States.

Let's take Florida Here is St. Augustine, by all odds the prettiest city in the United States. Mr. Flagler, who practically built the modern city, endeavored to make it a model. And it is —that is, the part that is seen by visitors. But in the jail, dirt as usual is king. And all the myriad vermin as usual pay homage. The quarters of the white prisoners are as bad as can be imagined. It is needless therefore to attempt to describe those occupied by the negroes. What a negro can expect when the quarters of the whites are so bad can be illustrated by a little incident which occurred while I was present in one of the jails in the south. A negro failed to turn off the water after he had used it to wash his hands, whereupon the jailer yelled to him, with the usual number of oaths considered necessary when talking to a negro: "Turn off that water, nigger! Don't you know that water costs more than niggers?"

The jail at Tampa, in addition to numberless other vicious features, is occasionally flooded by back water at high tide, due to the presence of open sewers in the jail. I have found such a situation by no means rare in other parts of the country. Like nine out of ten other Florida jails, it has no compulsory bathing rules, no segregation (except of the sexes and the white and black races), no examination of incoming prisoners to see if they are vermin-infested or sick, no exercise or recreation and no facilities for the care of insane prisoners. One thing it does have is an exceptionally large amount of vermin. Once again I call attention to the fact that many of the prisoners have never even been convicted.

There are not three jails in the state that have matrons, and not ten where even the sheriff's wife looks after the women prisoners. There are nearly always young boys in confinement in the various jails, and almost invariably they mingle with the older prisoners, there being not even a pretense of keeping them separate. Almost without exception, the jails lack hospital facilities, while the washing of the prisoners' clothing and the bedding

83

is something undreamed of.

There does not appear to be the slightest inclination on the part of charity organizations, individuals or the state to do anything at all for the prisoners, except to treat them with indifference and neglect.

For many years the City of Jacksonville has tolerated one of these crucibles of corruption, where prisoners of all classes are thrown promiscuously into the melting pot, there to be degraded, dissolved in decay and degeneracy, thoroughly mixed with these elements, and finally fused into the finished product labelled: "Guaranteed Criminal—Made in American Jails."

And so it goes all through Florida. At Key West, as in so many jails of the country, the loathsome "night bucket," as it is politely termed, is used. The night bucket, which we have met so often, is used in jails—there are hundreds of them—which have no toilet facilities or plumbing in the cells. They are emptied each morning. As they are made of iron and last for many years, and as so many jailers are not particularly concerned that they be kept as clean as possible, the atmosphere of such a jail will be apparent. These buckets stay in the cells all night, the prisoners breathing this foul air for a period of eight or ten hours. An obviously unnecessary and senseless procedure for destroying health, and promoting disease where it already exists. On the outside of the jail we have all sorts of organizations for fighting disease, and special efforts (and "drives" to finance them) are made to stamp out tuberculosis, while on the inside we do everything possible to increase disease, especially tuberculosis, which thrives on impure air, and then send it out to spread in the community.

Occasionally one does hear of a grand jury making a report concerning jail conditions which does not whitewash everybody and everything, but tells the truth as it sees it. Several years ago the grand jury of Birmingham, Alabama, made a report concerning the county jail at this place in which they stated about as follows.

"That the jail was obsolete and that, regardless of who manages it, it's no place to confine human beings, as the prisoners did not get sufficient air and exercise; that only two meals a day were served, one at seven-fifteen A. M. and the other at twelve-fifteen P. M., the interval between the second and the first meal on the following day being entirely too long; that the jail was unclean and unsanitary; that the discipline was largely administered by a Kangaroo Court composed of prisoners and that no prisoner could receive any privileges unless he was in good standing with this court."

I breathe a profound "amen" to everything the grand jury reported and feel that they were indeed very lenient. The sheriff admitted to me that the bed clothing had not been cleaned for many months. Here again strap iron bars were used, making the interior resemble perpetual dusk. As to the lack of air and exercise, mentioned by the grand jury, I can only say that, bad as it is, it is simply a matter of course in ninety-five percent of the jails in the United States.

86

The conditions got to be such a scandal that even the citizens demanded that some action be taken. It just happened that I was at the institution while an effort was being made to clean it. My work while with the Government took me into many vile places from which I emerged feeling "creepy" for many days. But I do not believe that I have ever seen such a sight as took place here. Cartload after cartload of an accumulation of every kind of waste matter which had been allowed to collect for years and years was taken from this jail.

The cellar of the institution was literally packed with it, where it defiled the air and made the entire place a noisome breeding ground for disease. The sheriff informed me that "sometime they intended to build a new jail." To use a popular expression, "that's what they all say."

In an effort to secure better accommodations for the federal prisoners, I began negotiations with the city officials to see if they would not take such prisoners in the city jail. But after looking at this institution, I decided to "let bad enough alone," as it was, if anything, more offensive than the other institution.

One trouble with the jails is that most of the jailers of the country do not know dirt when they see it. This appears to be particularly true in the south. On more than one occasion, upon insisting that the federal prisoners be given cleaner quarters, I have had jailers indignantly deny that their jail was unclean, notwithstanding the fact that I went around with them and pointed out the dirt on the floor, ran my hand over the blankets to show the black which came off, and otherwise tried to make them see what was before their eyes.

In Indiana, according to a recent report of the Board of State Charities, only ten of their ninety county jails are worthy of approval. This is just a little more than ten percent. Five or six of them are mentioned particularly as lacking in all sanitary features; two of them are so old that they have settled to an extent which prevents the locking devices from operating; while it is stated that in eight or ten of them "long confinement would be a serious menace to the health of the prisoners." Thirteen are mentioned as not having proper provisions for the segregation of the sexes and of juveniles. The last time I examined the jail at Indianapolis, a short time ago, I found the cells of the institution to be decidedly dirty. In addition the State Board finds the administration to be lax and the food insufficient.

There can be no excuse for community ignorance of these conditions. In the reports of the Board mentioned above they have been made public year after year—and year after year they have been ignored.

But the climax of criminal indifference is reached in Indiana's care of insane prisoners. Under the Indiana law insane persons must first be committed to the county jails until the necessary legal steps can be taken for commitment to a hospital, and room made for them there. The board itself declares:

"Some states have made such provision for their insane that they can be admitted at once to a state hospital. Indiana has not done this. Necessary legal steps for commitment (to a hospital) is often a slow and tedious process, *and all the time the patient's chances of ultimate recovery lessen.* Usually there are from fifty to seventy insane persons in the county jail at a time. *In the last ten years the whole number admitted has averaged 935 annually. This year, 1920, 892 insane were admitted.* (The italics are mine.)

Also it says:

"Attention is again called (note the "again") to the deplorable practice of caring for the insane in county jails. In several jails one or more insane were found. Seven insane men were found in the Madison County jail. *Several of them had been there for many months and one for two years.* These men were confined on the second floor *without supervision or special care. There was no provision for locking up any who became violent.*

In other words, during ten years there were 9,350 insane persons confined in the county jails of Indiana, as the Board itself says, many of them for months and even years at a time, with no attempt whatever made to treat them, and no adequate facilities even for restraining them. During this time "the patient's chances of ultimate recovery lessen." And if an insane person should die under such treatment? Under the law every man is held responsible for the natural and probable consequences of his acts. Is a state then permitted to engage freely in the very same acts for which it iso vigorously prosecutes the individuals composing it? It not only seems so; it is so!

CHAPTER V.

TREATMENT OF WOMEN.

The Factor of the Male Jailer—Unrestricted Looseness
—Girls at Gainesville—Demoralizing the Adolescent—
Mrs. O'Hare and the Missouri State Prison—Emma
Goldman—Bathing Rules—The "Hole"—The So-Called
Hospital—Homo-sexuality—Whipping Women—Virginia
State Penitentiary—Women as the Cause of Crime.

The conditions described so far generally relate to men, as has been noticed, no doubt. And the situations have so often called for superlatives that the reader probably feels sure he is acquainted with the worst by now. But just as there are many shades of black, and at the moment when we think we have found the darkest of all we come across another still a shade deeper in hue, so it is with the treatment of women in jails. This is blacker than many previous blacks. Such a state of affairs can be easily understood when it is realized that at all events male prisoners have to deal with male keepers, but that women are usually in charge of men, which brings a new factor into the situation.

Not ten percent of the jails in the United States employ matrons to care for the female prisoners. In a very few of the smaller places the wife of the jailer will look after them, but I repeat that, including this small number, not ten percent have any women attendants whatsoever.

In the remaining ninety percent, the male jailers have at all times free and unrestricted access to the women's quarters, and I have not once, nor a dozen times, but actually upon hundreds of occasions seen jailers walk through the women's quarters without even the formality of announcing their presence, taking it quite as a matter of course whether the women were fully dressed, half dressed, or scarcely dressed at all. I have on many occasions seen them walk through unconcernedly while the women were even engaged in performing their toilet. In such jails the women are absolutely at the mercy of the officials who can, if they desire, work their will upon them, be they submissive, reluctant or defiant. I do not say that the majority of jailers take advantage of this situation. To my knowledge some of them do. Only recently a case came to my attention in which a jailer hastily resigned following disclosures of undue familiarity with the female prisoners in his charge But whether they take advantage of the situation or not, the fact remains that all jailers where no matrons are employed are in a position to do so and that the women in these places have no one at all to whom they can turn for protection. This is not mentioned in the judge's sentence, either.

In the jail at Gainesville, Georgia, during the war, I saw eight or ten girls who walked around the jail with no clothing whatever except a very thin skirt. They were barefoot, and wore nothing at all above the waist. Not only the jailer, but also any of the town loafers who happened to wander in could easily see into the women's quarters, and the jailer walked in and out in pursuance of his duties in the same matter of fact way in which he walked around the quarters of the men. Both were indescribably filthy.

As a general rule women's quarters in most jails are in a little better condition than those of the men. This does not, by any stretch of the imagination, mean that the quarters are anything like they should be

The lack of segregation for younger prisoners, to which I have referred in connection with men, applies with equal force to the women. Girls of twelve and fourteen years of age are confined in the same room with abandoned prostitutes, and older women who have fallen into the very abyss of degradation. Some of these younger girls are by no means hardened or cursed with an incurable criminal propensity. There are among them many who would easily be amenable to suggestion and discipline. In

95

proper environment and with the exercise of a little care and patience (certainly not too high a price to pay for the reclamation of a human being) they would have developed into useful citizens.

Their minds still in the formative state which easily absorbs and retains impressions, they are thrown into the company of the most hardened women. They listen to the stories of crimes related with all the embellishments with which typical criminals, the vainest class on earth, love to surround their anecdotes; they absorb the sneers at virtue and morality, the mocking of truth, of love, of justice, of all the finer things which form the very cornerstone of civilized existence, and they emerge mentally polluted and beyond redemption, firmly convinced that every one is "crooked" and that those in jail are merely the few unfortunates who have been caught. Is it strange then that prisoners' aid societies and similar organizations feel discouraged in the face of repeated failures with girls of this class?

Nor are the quarters or the living conditions for women in some of the penitentiaries of the country what they should be. This brings to mind the Missouri State Prison where was confined Mrs. Kate Richards O'Hare. Mrs. O'Hare, with the possible exception of Emma Goldman, was the most widely known woman convicted under the special legislation enacted during the war. She, like Emma Goldman, served a sentence in the Missouri State Penitentiary at Jefferson City, and I went to that place to make an investigation of complaints which she had made concerning the treatment of women in this institution.

Mrs. O'Hare is a woman of vision and intelligence, and when she launched forth into a discussion of the conditions under which women lived in the Missouri Prison, and what should be done to change conditions, I found her very much worth listening to. She has an unusually dominating personality, and I recall vividly the contrast of disappointment which I felt upon meeting and talking with Emma Goldman, the noted anarchist, immediately after I had talked with Mrs. O'Hare. Two more dissimilar types it would be hard to imagine; Mrs. O'Hare tall, erect, intelligent-looking, and "alive" to her finger-tips; Emma Goldman short, squat, dull-looking, stooped shouldered and phlegmatic.

Before Mrs. O'Hare had been at the Missouri Prison many months her commanding personality asserted itself, and, following many bitter protests on her part, improvements were made. She made a number of criticisms, all of which I cannot vouch for, because information upon which some of them are based could only be obtained by living at the institution and absorbing the atmosphere. But I do know that many of the evils named in my report to which she called attention in a pamphlet addressed to the President, written after her release, do exist, or at any rate did until the time that her protests became so insistent and pressure which she brought to bear from the outside so great that the officials were forced to take action to remedy some of the most glaring abuses.

There was just one tub which was used by all the women whether they were diseased or well, and Mrs. O'Hare called attention to the fact that under threat of punishment, she was compelled to bathe after a woman who was in the last stage of syphilis. For punishment, the women were put into what is known in prisons as the "hole." The hole is a dark cell in which prisoners are usually kept until they promise obedience. The Missouri Prison is the only penitentiary which I have ever seen which did not furnish at least a sleeping board to prisoners confined in the hole. But here they had not even this convenience. Only one blanket was given them, and the women were compelled to sit and sleep on the cement floor, in utter disregard of their physical condition. There are times of course when a woman is particularly susceptible to colds, pneumonia, and other ills. But this fact made no difference whatever in the Missouri State Prison. The women went into the "hole" regardless. On page thirty-one of her pamphlet Mrs. O'Hare makes the following statement:

"Because of a protest I made to the Department of Justice in behalf of the Federal prisoners, Mr. Fishman, the Federal Inspector of Prisons, demanded that a wooden sleeping board be provided and this was done."

This statement is entirely correct, as I did tell the officials that I thought it was a disgrace and an outrage that women should be compelled to sleep, possibly for days at a time, on a cold cement floor.

The so-called hospital for the women was no hospital at all, but simply a bare room. It had absolutely no equipment, and I would not have known for what purpose the room was used if I had not asked the matron to show me the hospital, and been conducted to this room. It

100

illustrates better than anything I could say how an inexperienced person can be misled by institutional reports or statements concerning their equipment. The person being given this information would naturally have in mind the ordinary well equipped hospital, when as a matter of fact the actuality was nothing of the sort.

Mrs. O'Hare complains in her pamphlet of the appalling amount of homosexuality which exists in the women's section of the Missouri Prison, and states that in her opinion fully seventy-five per cent of the inmates are abnormal or subnormal. This figure is entirely too high, but Mrs. O'Hare was naturally led into such an exaggeration because, having. no previous personal knowledge of prisons, she was swept off her feet to find that such things existed. She was utterly amazed when I told her that homo-sexuality was a real problem in every prison. The presence of a large number of sub-normal and abnormal persons in a penitentiary is due entirely to the failure to study, classify and handle prisoners scientifically.

What will the women voters of America think when I tell them that in the Virginia State Penitentiary at Richmond they whip women for infractions of the rules. Colored women, you say? Yes, and white as well. And this, too, in a state where "chivalry" is so strong that any negro who is even suspected of relations with the most degraded white woman would be lynched without compunction.

The whippings are done by a male officer of the institution, and the women are required to remove their waists. In the warden's own words, the number of lashes given is "not less than ten nor more than thirty-nine." Nor is the practice of whipping women confined to Virginia. It exists in several other southern states.

At one time the Department of Justice contemplated using the Virginia

Penitentiary for female federal prisoners, and I went to Richmond to endeavor to make the necessary arrangements. In questioning the officials concerning various matters of administration I learned about the whipping of women. But the Warden positively declined to discontinue this practice when I told him I would not under any circumstances recommend the use of the institution unless it were stopped.

The accommodations for women in other respects are archaic and barbarous. The cell house used for women is very old and decidedly insanitary. The cells are small stone cages and except through a small door in front, have no ventilation whatsoever. They have neither wash basins nor toilets and the women use the atrocious "night bucket" for their personal convenience.

While we are on the subject of women it might not be amiss to rout that much exploited superstition that women are the cause of crime. Only a short

103

time ago the warden of a large eastern penitentiary aroused a great deal of comment by announcing to a woman's club that "a large percentage of the men in prison are there because of a woman."

This warden belongs to that class of untrained men who, perhaps prominent in some other field, go into prison work without an atom of previous training or experience. At the time he made this statement, he had been warden for only a few months. Like so many other new prison officials who have made similar superficial analyses, he was struck by the apparent phenomenon of 56 female prisoners to 906 male prisoners, and when taxed with the apparent superior morality of their sex by his women auditors, he immediately passed on the age-old explanation supplied by his own male wards. In so many words he said: "New prisoners invariably tell me their downfall is primarily due to a woman." In reply his women auditors promptly accused him, and in my opinion rightly so, of "falling for the old Adam stuff."

No, women are not the great cause of crime. They are the great excuse. Of course, such a thing as men blaming themselves alone for their own misdeeds is not to be thought of for a single moment. Before prohibition they blamed their crimes on drink. Now that liquor is abolished, they fall back on another old reliable which has been in service since the days of the Garden of Eden.

On the contrary, I can state without hesitancy that in a large percentage of cases men are the cause of crime in women. In the case of women, however, they are too "game" to blame the men. I have never had one woman tell me her downfall was caused by a man. But I have had hundreds of men tell me that their downfall was caused by a woman.

Concerning the wide discrepancy in the number of women and men criminals, in my opinion this is an apparent rather than a real discrepancy. To my mind, prostitution in women is the analogue of crime in men. Where a man is a criminal (using the word in its generally accepted sense) a woman is a prostitute. And certainly no one will contend that there are not as many, if not more, prostitutes in the United States than male criminals.

That prostitution in women is the analogue of crime in men is rather conclusively shown by the fact that, while the greatest percentage of criminality in men is between 25 and 35, the greatest percentage of criminality, other than prostitution, in women is between the ages of 45 and 55, when they are no longer able to make a living as prostitutes. And the reason why there are not as many women criminals (again using the word in its generally accepted sense) between the ages of 45 and 55 as there are men criminals between those ages, is that many prostitutes do not live that long.

CHAPTER VI.

NARCOTICS.

Parish Prison at New Orleans—The "Trusty" System —A Morphine Scandal—Creating Drug Addicts—Medically Sanctioned Traffic—Unspeakable Missouri—Eighteen Prisoners in Three Cells—Sick and Insane—A Hundred Years of Overcrowding—"We Sure Do Need One" —St. Louis and Kansas City—Smuggling Narcotics—Cocaine, Opium, Yenshee and Morphine—"Doing Your Bit on a Pill"—The Visitors' Screen—The Prison "Underground"—Detecting Drugs—Treatment of Drug Addicts.

Take the Parish Prison at New Orleans. This is called a prison, but is really a jail. From top to bottom it is filthy and has an odor which is just as obnoxious as it is inexcusable. If the place was ever cleaned, its appearance certainly does not indicate it. The entire institution is alive with bed bugs and vermin. In addition, when I last visited New Orleans, a comparatvely short time ago, it had a "trusty system" which included all the bad features of such a system and none of the good.

Practically all jails and penitentiaries

hard boiled guys

—that is, prisons—pick out certain prisoners who are given responsibilities and allowed privileges which the main body of prisoners does not receive. Generally speaking, it is the practice to choose as trusties men who have a greater degree of intelligence or education, and who have shown by their conduct that they can be trusted to perform competently various official tasks and not abuse accompanying privileges. But in the Parish Prison it has been the custom to choose for trusties the very toughest of the "hard boiled guys," those who can be depended upon to use their fists, or the sticks with which they are thoughtfully provided, with the greatest efficiency and dispatch. When I was there the prisoners were turned out in the yard at noon to be fed, at which time these trusties, armed with their sticks, kept order, and if a prisoner attempted to obtain more food than the trusty thought he was entitled to a neat blow on the head or back soon convinced him that, like Oliver

108

Twist, he was not supposed to ask for more. Nor was the jailer at the time himself too dignified to preserve order in this manner. He was seen to strike a prisoner over the back with a stick, and later admitted it to me.

But it is not only for the disgustingly dirty condition of the institution and the clubbing of the prisoners that this jail is entitled to dishonorable mention. It possesses a further claim to distinction for the manner in which its morphine addicts have been treated. I began an investigation of this matter after it was noticed that the Government was being billed by a local firm of druggists for a large amount of morphine tablets, these bills showing the amount of such tablets opposite the name of the prisoners for whom they were intended. Now, there are several methods of treating morphinism, one of the oldest being what is known as the "reduction treatment." This means, as its name implies, simply reducing the amount of morphine given each day until the patient can get along without any. For instance, if a prisoner is taking ten grains a day when he is received in jail, some doctors reduce the quantity one quarter grain each day, so that the second day the patient will get nine and three-quarters; the third, nine and a half; the fourth, nine and a quarter; and so on, until he is getting none at all. This is the system *supposed* to be used at the Parish Prison. Actually they had a system of their own which, even if it didn't cure any prisoners, certainly redounded to the financial benefit of the local drug firm in question. I found that several prisoners had been receiving enormous quantities of morphine tablets within a period of four or five days, these quantities of course being so enormous as to render absurd any idea that the prisoners receiving them were being given the reduction treatment. On questioning, the physician employed and paid by the Government to treat its federal prisoners made a statement which, for complacent indifference to the health of the prisoners and for spineless acquiescence to the dictation of the jail officials, it would be hard to equal anywhere.

It seems that the jail officials had insisted that all prescriptions should be filled by one local firm of druggists, in spite of the fact that this concern could not fill the prescriptions which the physician gave for tablets containing varying quantities of morphine, but had one stock tablet containing a set percentage of morphine. The doctor admitted without reservation that he knew these stock tablets were utterly worthless as far as their effecting a cure was concerned. He blandly followed this admission with the almost unbelievable statement that he had never yet cured any prisoner of the morphine habit who was confined in the Parish Prison, since the tablets he was getting simply enabled them to continue the habit.

But as if this were not enough, it was

also found that prisoners were actually contracting the morphine habit after coming to the Parish Prison. One prisoner, named Culbertson, had been confined to the jail for more than two months before he received any "treatment" for morphinism. When asked concerning this case, the doctor not only said it was possible that Culbertson had contracted this habit while in confinement, but cheerfully admitted that it was very probable. He stated that he knew some of the prisoners received enormous quantities of these stock morphine tablets, and that there was no question at all in his mind that these prisoners had distributed them indiscriminately to such other prisoners as were able to pay for them. In other words, what the prisoners did was to conduct an open traffic in morphine tablets prescribed by the prison doctor, this traffic being carried on with the tacit acquiescence of the jail officials, if not indeed with their active connivance.

It is almost needless to add that I found the United States government was paying almost three times as much for these preparations as they should have. The only defense which the doctor made of his conduct was that he "did not wish to antagonize anyone at the jail." Of course the creation and development of regiments of drug addicts to be turned loose from time to time on an unsuspecting world was perfectly all right. At least it didn't arouse anyone's antagonism. For the doctor well knew that no one outside of the jail would know what was going on since, as I have said, the public does not take an active interest in the jails, but thus unknowingly acquiesces in the increase of danger to itself. Up to this day, people living within a block of the Parish Prison are ignorant of this breeding place of drug addicts in their midst, as this situation has never before been made public. Of course, no one could expect an individual, occupied with his private affairs, to take upon

113

himself an investigation of every public institution which he thought was not being properly conducted. But private individuals could see to it that competent inspectors (extra-local, if necessary, so as to avoid political or other entanglements) with authority to make necessary changes, made periodical investigations of their institutions and made their findings public. In this way, the public could at least know what is going on.

Following my investigations the physician for the federal prisoners was "relieved," and another physician appointed in his place. In addition, I had the Department discontinue the use of this institution as far as possible, and use the House of Detention instead. But, as I have said, the Government has no jurisdiction whatever over the state prisoners and had no authority to correct this condition as far as they were concerned.

Now, on to Missouri. From St. Louis on the east to Kansas City on the west, I doubt if there are five county jails which could be described as being even in fairly decent condition. Out of one hundred and fifteen county jails in the state at least a hundred reek with the odors of leaky plumbing, or what is far worse, odors which result from having practically no plumbing. Almost without exception from one end of the state to the other they are unspeakably dirty and unsanitary, swarming with vermin, frightfully overcrowded and generally so atrocious that it is hard to believe they are meant to house humans. Classification of any kind, except of the sexes and the negro and white races is an unheard-of thing.

"Cells are dark, unsanitary, and unfit for anyone to live in. Therefore the rule to permit all prisoners to mingle freely in the open spaces between cells. Not long ago I visited a jail in one of the wealthiest counties of the State, where eighteen prisoners were occupying three cells, and near these in a corner of the cell was an insane prisoner who had been confined five days. Of the eighteen prisoners, six were boys under the age of eighteen. Black and white, sick and well, the prisoners waiting trial were all crowded together. The cells were so dark that I stumbled over two

115

> boys lying on the floor. They were in the same cell with a sick man, and but a few days before a man had died there with pneumonia, presumably contracted in the jail. Under such conditions these prisoners had lived for weeks with an air space of 67 cubic feet that should have been 500."

This is from a report of their own State Board of Charities and Corrections made in the early part of 1914. 1914 you say! Yes, and the same conditions are still existing today in the vast majority of the jails of the State. The same conditions, with the still further deterioration of nine years' use!

A typical instance is the Jasper County jail at Carthage. I have a photograph which shows the frightful condition of overcrowding about which I have already spoken, and which I have seen in hundreds of jails throughout the United States. The photographer who took this picture was William Weaver, and his widow who sent me the photograph wrote me in the latter part of 1921 as follows

"Mr. Weaver was turnkey at this county jail for six years, and I know what I am saying. This picture does not show it half as bad as it is or was then. The jail was built in 1817, and built to accommodate about twenty-eight or thirty prisoners, *and Mr. Weaver's average was eighty-five the six years he was there.* I have kept this photograph hoping it would help us to get a new jail for Jasper County. We sure do need one, oh so bad."

The italics are mine. Now understand that when the statement is made that the average was eighty-five, it does not seem that eighty-five was the maximum. There doubtless are many days when the number runs considerably over a hundred. And packed into a space designed to hold twenty-eight or thirty.

St. Louis and Kansas City afford an interesting contrast. The jail at St. Louis is new and unusually well kept. But Kansas City, which takes such a vast amount of pride in her increasing population, the number and size of her office buildings, the growth of her industries, her bank clearings and other advantages, takes none whatever in her jail. Now the jail at Kansas City is not by any means the worst in the country, but it is

117

far, and very far, from being even fair. It is old and gloomy. It is poorly lighted and ventilated. It reeks with disinfectant. The quarters occupied by the white prisoners are not clean, while those of the negroes are particularly dirty. The personnel is far from being of a high type. And as in ninety-five percent of the other jails throughout the country, the jailers have not the remotest idea of sanitation or hygiene, or any sense of responsibility for the moral welfare of the human material with which they are entrusted.

When I see in the same state such a pleasing contrast as the jail at St. Louis makes to the usual run of the others, I cannot help thinking how simple a thing it would be in reality for all jails to be made and kept decently habitable instead of the decent ones being the rare exception. In reviewing the entire United States, one would think indeed that for a community to maintain a decent, habitable jail, it must require a superhuman effort. But when I come to the measures

118

necessary for remedying conditions, I think you will agree that after all the main requirements are common sense and some intelligent attention to the matter.

The jail at Kansas City, like the one at New Orleans, brings narcotics to mind. Upon one occasion. the bills which the Government was receiving from the Kansas City jail for medical attendance on federal prisoners became so high that I went to Kansas City to investigate. The physician employed to treat federal prisoners told me he was having unusual trouble in the treatment of morphine addicts because, according to his own statement, "the jail is a sieve through which narcotics pour." I cannot vouch for the entire accuracy of his statement, but upon discussing this matter with one of the jailers I was informed that scarcely a week passed during which efforts were not made by friends of prisoners to smuggle narcotics into them. Just a few days

morphine

before I arrived there, the friend of a prisoner brought him a box of ice cream. The jailer stuck a spoon in it and dug out a large package of morphine.

The narcotic habit is one of the worst evils with which every penal institution has to contend, and even the conscientious jail official has difficulty enough in preventing it. He is met at every turn by a cunning and cleverness on the part of the prisoner which would take the latter far along the road to success if it were only applied in the right direction. The extent of the habit in the United States is amazing, and there are many indications of a recent tremendous increase in the number of addicts. Morphine and other narcotics have, of course, the advantage of not being nearly so bulky as liquor, which naturally makes the drug traffic much more difficult to stop. In the jails and prisons are concentrated a large number of the worst addicts, who are utterly lacking in will power and unable to help themselves.

120

The narcotics used by prisoners include not only morphine, but also a number of other drugs. In fact, they will use any substance which will give them the desired "kick" or "jolt." These drugs include cocaine, heroin (a narcotic which is usually snuffed up the nose), opium, yenshee (the residue of smoked opium), and in fact anything they can obtain which has any narcotic effect whatever. I have even found in some cases that prisoners will eat the crust remaining in the bowl of a tobacco pipe after it has been used for a long time. They claim that they get quite a "kick" from this.

The use of bay rum, where the prison or jail has a barber shop, is not at all uncommon. In some cases they use cannabis indica, more commonly known as hashish, the use of which is common throughout India and far eastern countries. Cannabis indica causes very pleasant color sensations and practically inhibits the will from any kind of action. Strangely enough, the Harrison Anti-

Narcotic Act does not place any restriction on its sale. It can be obtained in almost any drug store. It is often used as a base for corn cures, and I know personally one man who has frequently purchased it, telling the druggist that he wanted to use it for corns.

The narcotic addicts are known among the prisoners as "hopheads" and "snowbirds," while the use of drugs is rather tersely described by them as "doing your bit on a pill." A "deck" is a small package of opium; a "stem" is a pipe; and a "layout," a complete equipment for the use of narcotics. Their methods for obtaining narcotics while confined are as ingenious as they are surprising. One of the more common practices is for them to endeavor to have their friends or relatives slip the drug to them concealed in some article of food upon visiting day. This is a trick which every experienced official knows, and usually every precaution is taken to guard against it. But in spite of such precautions, there are very few institutions in the United States in which narcotics are not introduced at some time. I have on many occasions seen apples, oranges and bananas loaded with morphine. They had been so cleverly hollowed out and put together again that it was almost impossible to detect it, and there is no question but that on many occasions the less experienced officials have these tricks "put over" on them.

Many years ago it was thought that the practice of introducing such contraband articles could be prevented by the use of what have come to be known as visitors' screens. A visitor's screen is a screen of heavy wire with an extremely fine mesh through which the prisoner and his visitor must converse with each other, the prisoners sitting on one side and the visitor on the other. In spite of such screens friends of prisoners still managed to slip them narcotics. It was then decided by some jails to put up a double screen with an intervening space of two or three feet. But if the officials thought that this was going to deter the more resourceful among the prisoners' friends they were very much mistaken, for by the use of wires and long narrow sticks the prisoners still managed to obtain some.

Of course many articles which prisoners are allowed to receive are sent to them through the mail. These packages are supposed to be examined by the officials, but here too new tricks are tried which very often succeed. Large quantities of cocaine have been discovered in the heels of slippers, which had been removed, hollowed out and replaced. Belts and the hems of handkerchiefs have been loaded with it, and in one institution a quantity of opium sufficient to satisfy an addict for many years was found concealed in a freight car switched into the prison yard. Investigation revealed that a friend of the prisoner for whom it was intended had placed it there after ascertaining that the car contained goods destined to the institution. The prisoner's friend has "tipped him off" in advance through the "under ground" communication system, and the prisoner expected to obtain it while in the yard during one of the recreation periods.

Some institutions do not have screens and prisoners meet their relatives and friends on visiting days in the presence of an officer, the primary purpose of his presence being to see that no contraband is passed. However, the wisest and most sophisticated guards are often fooled. A wife has more than once been caught dropping morphine down the blouse of her prisoner husband while greeting him with an affectionate hug, and even transferring small packages from her mouth to his while kissing him.

At the Federal Penitentiary at Leavenworth, Kansas, it was found upon one occasion that there was a considerable quantity of cocaine somewhere in the institution. Prisoners were frequently seen under its influence. After a patient investigation lasting many weeks the secret was revealed. It was found that an unusual large number of handkerchiefs were being received as gifts by one of the prisoners who was a well known "snowbird." Finally it was discovered that each of them had a small ink mark in one of the corners, and a further investigation brought to light the fact that these handkerchiefs had been dipped in cocaine and then carefully ironed. The mark in the corner notified the "snowbird" that it was "loaded." The prisoner would dip it in a glass of water and allow the cocaine to settle to the bottom, after which he drained the water off. He was not only using the cocaine himself, but was actually selling some of the handkerchiefs to the other prisoners in exchange for tobacco, which is the money or medium of exchange of every penal institution. Some of his customers would not even bother to remove the cocaine but would simply suck the handkerchiefs, literally "chewing the rag," as one prison wit aptly remarked.

In the case of another "snowbird" a most curious thing apparently took place. This fellow was being given the reduction treatment internally, yet was continually troubled with the abscesses which invariably follow the use of an unclean needle. The effect of morphine is considerably greater and quicker if taken with a hypodermic needle than through the mouth, and even when receiving treatment the fiend prefers it hypodermically. As the physician himself stood by the bedside while the treatment was being administered internally he was extremely puzzled to know just what and how the prisoner was injecting hypodermically. A close watch was kept for several days. And this is what transpired. As soon as the prisoner felt himself safely alone he would transfer the drug from his mouth where he had held it all the time, to a syringe and inject it. His syringe was improvised out of the glass barrel of a fountain pen filler, some paraffin, and a small hypodermic needle. He melted the paraffin, which he had obtained from the cracks of the hospital floor, with a match and used it to stick the needle to the barrel. With the drug supplied by the physician, his "dope" outfit was complete.

And it is just as necessary to examine closely the prisoner's mail for drugs as it is to examine their packages. A small quantity of cocaine is often placed by a prisoner's friend under the postage stamp of the letter which he sends him, or in a paper pocket made inside the envelope. The "trusties" too, whose duties take them outside the institution, must be watched. Every penitentiary has some of these "outside trusties." Frequent "fanning" or "frisking" (as the prisoner designates searching) of the trusties themselves is necessary if they are to be kept from bringing in narcotics. Very often prisoners obtain it through teamsters and other civilians whose duties take them inside the institution. And I am sorry to say that it is even necessary in a greater number of cases than one would think to watch some of the guards as much as the prisoners. Frequently I have had to cause the dismissal of officers who had permitted themselves to be used as a channel between the prisoners and the outside world. This is of course the most difficult to detect of all methods of introducing contraband. The foregoing, and other similarly secret channels constitute the prison "underground."

Prisoners display even more ingenuity in hiding narcotics after they are obtained than they do in smuggling them in. They carry it on their persons in the most unexpected places, often hiding it successfully in their ears, under their arm pits, in small rubber sacks in their mouths, strapped to the instep with adhesive tape, under their thighs, and in their hair. In fact, there is no part of their bodies which is spared the uses of concealment. The experienced "screw" (guard) will "fan" every inch of their bodies. And no contempt in the world is greater than that which a prisoner has for the "screw" who does not know how to properly "frisk" him. That is, for the guard who fails to prevent the prisoner from "holding out on him."

The lengths which the drug addict prisoners go to get some of their favorite "dope" are not difficult to understand when one has seen the heart breaking condition in which some of the addicts are received. A physician usually prescribes one eighth of a grain at a time to a suffering patient. He uses a quarter of a grain only in rather extreme cases of intense suffering. So it will mean something to you when I say that some of these prisoners have developed the habit to such an extent that they are taking as high as sixty grains a day. The use of ten, fifteen or twenty grains is not at all uncommon, and many of them will take other narcotics at the same time. I have seen men whose normal weight was 150 and 160 pounds weigh 85 or 90 pounds when they were received in jail. One case which particularly impressed itself upon me was that of a young man who had given himself so many injections in the arm that his flesh had atrophied from the wrist to the shoulder. It was like bone, and so hard that it was impossible to push a needle in it. He would make injections in his shoulder, back and stomach.

When the drug is taken away from them without any compensatory treatment, the torture they go through is indescribable, and even with such treatment they suffer considerably. I have on many occasions seen them lying on the floor of their cells screaming in agony. In some cases they could be heard a block away. They will butt their heads against the bars and throw themselves around in a positive frenzy of suffering. In the Cook County Jail at Chicago upon one occasion I saw a woman prisoner in this desperate condition. It was almost impossible to keep her dressed, for in her agony she would tear her clothes to shreds.

To take drugs suddenly away from such creatures without giving them some compensatory treatment is to plunge them into hell, yet in a great many institutions the drug is taken away from the prisoner immediately and nothing whatever, except possibly some mild sedative, is given. This is because in many of the jails of the country, particularly the smaller ones, the local physicians have no knowledge whatever concerning the treatment of these unfortunates. Their ignorance of such matters is astounding. Fully seventy-five percent of them have never even heard of the Towne-Lambert treatment, the father of all narcotic treatments. The more modern physicians now use a treatment the base of which is hyoscin. A prisoner placed under this drug for forty-eight hours or so loses his taste entirely for narcotics and undergoes practically no suffering. I am very much in favor of taking the drug absolutely away, but by all means giving some treatment to relieve the intense suffering which follows.

CHAPTER VII.

"TAKING THE VINEGAR OUT OF 'EM."

Take Texas. Out of this immense
area, I have seen only three places, Dallas, Fort Worth and San Antonio, which
have clean and modern institutions. Even
Fort Worth for many years and up until
a very short time ago tolerated an antiquated old building which, like the jail
at Cleveland, was so thoroughly saturated with dirt that it was impossible to
keep it clean. The cells had no toilets,
and night buckets were used.

The jails at Laredo, Corpus Christi,
Brownsville and Houston are in but
fairly good condition, while that at Gal-

veston is dirty and full of vermin.

Waco is in a class by itself. The last time I was there I visited the jail at noon on an unusually bright day. Looking into the cells, it was actually impossible to distinguish the features of the prisoners for a distance of more than three or four feet. The same irritating stupidity so generally shown in the construction of jails was here very evident. Instead of making the fronts of the cells of bar iron, so as to admit as much light and air as possible, they were made of strap iron, running both up and down and from side to side, leaving a mesh of about an inch. It was out of the question for a prisoner to read, even on the brightest day, without ruining his eyesight, so that, since the prisoners are kept in idleness (as in all jails with few exceptions) they are denied here even this small boon to help pass the time away when they are fortunate enough to have something to read.

I was reminded of what an old deputy

marshal had told me down in the Indian Territory years ago. Discussing a fight which he had had while he was arresting a prisoner, and the refusal of the prisoner to make a confession, he said, "Well, I'll leave him in jail for a few days and then talk to him. Loafing around the jails sure do take the vinegar out of 'em." I quite agree with him. It sure do! Such a jail as the one at Waco, "takes out of 'em" every ounce of physical, mental and moral vinegar.

Most jails make at least some pretense of keeping the women's quarters just a bit better than those of the men. No such chivalrous instinct found place in the breast of the jailer at Waco. The women's quarters were not as bad as the men's—they were worse. In showing me through, the jailer explained with a great deal of pride that juveniles were kept separated from the older and more hardened prisoners. This "separation" was a cell on the first floor which permitted the juveniles both sight and sound of the older prisoners. When I commented upon the fact that placing four prisoners in a cell, as the jailer said it was frequently necessary to do, appeared to greatly overcrowd the institution, he explained that "msot of the prisoners prefer to sleep on hte floor." And this is undoubtedly true, which can be understood easily after a single glance at the condition of the bedding. I do not believe that there is a pig, horse, or steer in Texas that does not have far better living accommodations than the men and women who are unfortunate enough to be confined at this place.

At Waco again the Government is confronted with the necessity under the present circumstances of continuing the use of what was known to be a thoroughly unfit institution.

I think of Arkansas. The one bright spot is Fort Smith, where the jail is in fairly good condition Throughout the state, it is the old story of criminal neglect and callous indifference. In Texarkana there is a bath tub but never any hot water. Dirt reigns here. The jail at Berryville is a horror, and at a dozen other towns in the State conditions are as bad.

In striking contrast to this, not only in location but in cleanliness are the jails of New Hampshire. Like in many New England institutions the jails here are kept clean. But like them and most others, they are afflicted with two outstanding evils—the complete idleness of the prisoners and the practice of confining two in a cell, which cannot do other than create greater opportunities for homo-sexuality than already exist.

I believe the jails of Oklahoma, both those in the county towns and those in the cities to be as thoroughly unfit, measured by every standard of comparison, as those of any state in the country. In the old territorial days, as long ago as 1906, I visited many of the jails in this state, which then comprised both Oklahoma and Indian territory. Even at that

138

time some of them would have been
scorned by a prairie dog; and the fact is
that a large number of them are still in
use at the present day. Since statehood,
I have visited some of the jails of Oklahoma on several different occasions and
each time found them just a little worse
than they had been on my previous visit.

I have before me the report of Oklahoma's own Commissioner of Charities
and Corrections. The Board inspected
177 jails in the state, including both city
and county institutions. It does not give
detailed accounts, but merely states
whether a jail had been condemned and
whether it is considered good, bad or
medium Out of the 177 jails there are
probably 50 which the board asserts are
in "good condition." The balance are
marked either medium or bad or condemned. From my knowledge of conditions existing in Oklahoma jails, particularly the larger ones, I am much inclined to believe that the board has given

the institutions the benefit of every doubt.

The county jail at Muskogee is marked "conditions bad." A fair characterization would be "conditions awful." It is seldom that I have seen a worse institution.

The Board states that in McAlester, conditions are "not good." Again it is lenient in its criticism.

"General conditions not good" is applied to the jail at Ardmore. "General conditions frightfully bad" should be said of this institution, which has always tried hard to vie with the worst in the State. Similarly mild criticisms are made of many other places in the state where I know conditions to be exceedingly bad.

The jail at Guthrie is condemned by the Board. I visited this jail in the old territorial days and even then it was only suitable for bats or owls.

To go through the report of the State Board is indeed a revelation In many cases all the institutions in entire counties, including the county jail, several city jails and the county poor farm are described as either "very bad," "not good," or "condemned." This, coupled with the tendency of the Board previously mentioned to give every institution a little more than it is actually entitled to, will convey some idea of what it means to be confined in a jail in this State, and of how bad a jail needs actually be before it is condemned.

As a matter of fact, conditions in jails must indeed become unbelievably intolerable before a new one is constructed. And one thing I wish to call attention to is that almost without exception when a decision is reached to build a new institution, it is invariably due to the growth of the community which has so increased the jail population as to make large quarters absolutely necessary from the point of view of numbers. The fact that prisoners may be living in the most loathsome surroundings amid conditions that

141

cannot do other than breed disease and crime is never taken into consideration as a reason for building a new institution. It is not the last thing thought of; it is simply never thought of at all. This is no general conclusion, but can be proven by dozens of striking instances. I will give just a few of them.

At Danville, Illinois, although the following conditions had been existing year in and year out a half century or more, it was not until a few years ago that a new jail was built.

The south section of the first floor is a small dark room containing a cage of five cells and a narrow corridor. The cage and the cell door are built of closely set bars. The cage corridor extends the length of the cells. The cells are solid iron and are placed back to back with the cells of the north section.

The cells are so dark that it is almost impossible to see what is in them. There are wall cots in some. In others, the prisoners are compelled to sleep on mattresses on the floor. There are three men to each narrow cell. The mattresses and blankets are old, very dirty and filled with vermin.

The walls of the cage and the room are horribly defaced and have not been whitewashed or painted for a long time.

142

Small vegetable cans are used for night buckets. There are only two night buckets that do not leak, the men said. The tin vegetable cans are uncovered. There is a toilet and a tub at the end of the corridor. The men are locked in their cells at six o'clock and have no access to the toilet until six o'clock in the morning.

The men said that the rats and vermin make the cells unbearable. They complained very bitterly of the drinking water. They get the water from the faucets and they say that the water for drinking is warm and the water for washing is cold.

The men were unshaven and their clothing was untidy. As changes of clothing or underclothing are not provided by the county, few of the men can keep clean. They wash their own clothes in the water which they say is not hot enough to secure cleanliness and clothing has to be dried in a dark cage.

Separate towels are not provided and healthy men must use the same towels as men infected with gonorrhea, syphilis, tuberculosis or other contagious diseases.

There is certainly nothing amusing about the above, every word of which is true, but I cannot help smiling at the last paragraph regarding separate towels. The jails which provide any towels at all, either separate, community or paper, or any other kind, are so few in number that one could almost recite them from memory. There is not one jail in five hundred where towels are furnished. The men are forced to dry themselves with toilet paper, newspaper, any rags they can find, or simply leave themselves to the mercy of the air.

A towel in most jails is an unheard of luxury, a luxury like having music with your meals, as they have at some penitentiaries in the country where there are prisoner bands. At one time I was trying to "cheer up" a prisoner in jail who was soon to be removed to the penitentiary at Leavenworth to serve a sentence. I talked at length on the merits of the place, telling him as a "clincher" that they had music with their meals, to which he replied, "Yes, but what I want to know is, do they have meals with their music?"

It all depends I suppose on what a man considers a luxury. Now, the average man would not consider it a luxury to find a mouse in his food, as did a prisoner in an institution which I happened to be visiting some years ago. To shame the steward, who was standing in the dining room, he held the mouse up by the tail in full view of everyone. But the steward said to him, "Put it down, Johnson. I haven't enough to go 'round."

Peoria is another city which for fifty-five years tolerated a crucible of crime and pestilence dignified with the name of jail, at last building a new one when the congestion of prisoners became too great to be longer tolerated. And lest you think that I may have looked at the jails which I have described through darkened glasses and with a view to making them appear as black as possible, I am again going to quote you from reports made by others. As long ago as 1915 Mr. A. L. Bowen, Secretary of the Illinois State Charities Commission, had this to say about Peoria:

> Fifty years ago a contractor sealed up an impervious roof and a boiler maker riveted impenetrable steel plate, punctured by small holes, as in a collander, over the narrow slits in the walls of a stone and iron building. The Peoria County jail was complete; it was mob proof.
>
> For fifty years not a ray of God's sunlight has penetrated these stone chambers. In the sun's annual course his benign face, on a few days,

145

comes squarely in front of the iron barred and boilerplated window slits on one side of the building; a modest, trepidating, slender little messenger ventures in through one of the tiny apertures and dances for a moment on the cold flags of the corridor floor, but never peeps into a cell; then is off to more congenial abodes.

For fifty years this Hole of Calcutta has been a festering breeding place of moral and physical plague. In a continuously growing stream, year after year, corruption and pestilence have flowed from this spot through the high-ways and by-ways of the community. There thousands of our unfortunate fellows have jostled; some have been gonorrheal, some syphilitic, many have been infected with body vermin. There has been the confirmed criminal, the repeater, steeped in his knowledge and love of crime, the old petty offender, the young first offender whom misfortune and temptation have combined to break in an unguarded hour, the moral degenerate, the sexual pervert; these have all mingled and associated in close contact, the bad always corrupting the good, the good seldom influencing the worse.

Of the total number incarcerated in this jail in these fifty years, probably forty or fifty per cent either were not indicted, or, if indicted, some were not convicted on trial. Under our theory of justice all the men who had been thrown in this jail were presumed to be innocent until, through the processes of law, they were determined to be guilty of offense.

Leaving out of the question the rights of those who were found guilty of crime, what shall we say of the injustice and the wrongs done by detention in this indescribable place, to this large percentage of men who were not only innocent by presumption, but were actually declared so on trial?

In one corner . . . is the lone bath tub, in which is fought, with indifferent results, an unequal battle between physical cleanliness and human vermin. This is a dual purpose bath-tub; for while not attempting to cleanse the skin of man, it is doing its level best to launder his dirty linen.

The cells were constructed as far from light and air as it was possible to get them.

In the darkest corner . . . is an old toilet which violates both State and City health regulations and all principles of scientific plumbing.

Four long windows, heretofore denominated slits, look down upon each corridor. In the clear these windows are about sixteen inches wide and ten feet long and fourteen inches in depth through the stone walls. They are so high above the floor that a man must stand on a chair to reach the bottom. The holes in the boiler plate are about three quarters of an inch in diameter.

Each cell is four feet wide, seven feet deep and seven feet high, giving it 196 cubic feet of air space inside measurements. It contains an iron cot on which is a matress and certain covering; a combination cuspidor and night bucket complete the outfit.

Up in one corner furthest from the door is a five inch opening covered by a finely punctured piece of boiler plate, and below it, just above the floor, a similar ventilating device. Even if this primitive circulatory system did work in practice, as it was expected to, it would be wholly inadequate to change the cell air. But it does not work. No one present could tell me when it did work. In the long years since its construction it doubtless has filled and clogged with dust and dirt.

Now imagine, if you can, a man—what matter it who or what he be, but a man—sleeping in any comfort or decency in a hole of 196 cubic feet, hewed out of solid rock, with an iron grated door in front and so located as to be denied both light and air. Imagine further his filthy matress steeped in disinfectant and possibly alive with ver-

147

min, and on the floor by his side an open bucket in which all calls of nature, in ten hours, have been answered. And then remember that this hole has been occupied every night for fifty years, its stagnant air reeking with vile odors, its corners and edges lodged with vermin and the dirt of the years, its walls never touched by the sun's blessed light. If you can picture to yourself some of these things, you may possibly conceive an idea of the Peoria County jail.

Twelve or fifteen feet above the floor and attached to the outside wall in each corridor is a pipe forty feet long, to which are fixed fourteen powerful tungsten lamps which burn day and night, year in and year out. During my visit I shut these off to determine whether any natural light penetrated through the windows. In one corridor it was impossible to distinguish forms. In the other corridor, which was on the sunny side, I could determine figures but not features.

The equipment of the jail is in keeping with the surroundings. The mattresses on the cots are of the cheapest grade. They are used for six months and then thrown away. It does not require a long time for them to become filthy. During their six months of life in the jail they receive frequent inundations of disinfectant, which has the merit of substituting one vile odor for another; and after a short time their parasitical inhabitants become immune to it and appear to whet their appetite upon it.

There are no sheets, no pillows. Contagion and infection may be communicated from man to man by contact with these dirty mattresses. During the day the cots and mattresses which have been used in the corridors at night are piled up in one of the cells, without the gracious touch of fresh air and sunshine. The corridors are almost devoid of chairs and stools. The men sit upon upturned buckets and other improvisations and play cards upon their knees.

The common drinking cup is present.

At night when I entered the cell house the odors of disinfectant combined with foul air from sixty-six inmates, were staggering. All windows on one side are closed tight.

The "Kangaroo Court" prevails and is responsible for much of the discipline among the prisoners. The State Charities Commision has condemned this institution. It has few, if any, valid arguments in its favor. Its abolition would be a contribution to good morals in the end.

About the only comment fitting to close this report is this: To confine one man in this jail, no matter what his crime or his condition in society, would be wrong, but to confine sixty, or seventy or eighty men in so small a space, with all the evils, disabilities and horrors which are apparent to any eye that will look, is a crime against humanity and against the community that cries out for justice.

Again I say "Amen." I have visited this institution on several occasions, and know that every word is true. Mr. Bowen's report is well written indeed and shows quite a grasp of language, but I should like to take him around outside of Illinois, show him "some jails I have met," and then see if his vocabulary is equal to a description of them.

The Greenville County jail, at Greenville, S. C., is another striking example

149

of what is going on all over the country in "respectable" communities. For forty-five years a miniature Siberia made history unheeded in Greenville's midst. Then came an exposure, with the press now all agog, making first page stories out of the conditions. Then silence. And for five years more a "respectable" community winked at official deafness to the pleas of the sheriff until the *number* of the prisoners, not their welfare, forced the building of a new jail. This was five years ago. Before that Greenville made a fourth to the other three worst jails.

And because the other jails of the state are not far behind what Greenville was five years ago, I shall describe somewhat the little Siberia of fifty years' undisturbed standing.

It had no windows at all. In the back wall of each cell (which was also the outside wall) there were three slits, each about five inches wide, making an open space of about fifteen inches all told. There was absolutely no protection from

150

the weather, the temperature of the jail being at all times about what it was on the outside, or possibly a little lower, due to the absence of the sun. These openings created a current of air in the winter which swept through the cells and literally froze the occupants.

At this season the prisoners endeavored to protect themselves in a measure by tearing the blankets into strips and placing them over these openings. There were only two small stoves which were utterly inadequate and I do not believe they made a difference in temperature of two degrees. On one floor was a so-called "bath-room," but as the jail had no plumbing, a prisoner who desired to bathe had to heat the water on the stove bucket by bucket, dipping the water out of the tub again with a bucket after he finished his bath, as there was no other way to empty the tub. It was, of course, impossible to get all the water out in this fashion, and there was a constant accumulation of sediment and an inch or more of the filthiest water imaginable in the bottom of the tub. Iron toilets were in use, but as there was no up-to-date plumbing it was necessary to flush the toilets by throwing buckets of water into them.

There were two bunks in each cell, two men sleeping on a bunk. When the jail was crowded as many as six men slept in a cell. The jail was small and could not possibly accommodate more than twenty prisoners at a time. But at times of holding court, as many as fifty and sixty United States prisoners alone were confined there, to say nothing of any number of state prisoners. The sheriff informed me that at such times the jail was so frightfully over-crowded that there was not sufficient room for all the men to lie down, even using the floor space of the cells and corridors, so that many of the men stood up all night and did not get one wink of sleep. There were no facilities what-ever for keeping the younger prisoners separated from the older, although the sheriff informed me that he usually had two or three young boys who had been employed in one of the numerous cotton mills around the city. At the time of one of my visits there was a young boy twelve years of age in the jail with the rest of the men, many of whom were of the most debased and degenerate type. The corruption of body and mind which must inevitably follow such criminal negligence as this requires no further comment.

I have often been asked why, if conditions in the jails are as foul as have been described, the prisoners themselves do not make complaints either while they are confined or after their release. But in the majority of cases, the average prisoner, when once he is out, lets the thing slide, often from sheer inability to get a hearing, no matter how harshly or unfairly he has been treated. While still in jail most of the prisoners are afraid to complain because experience has taught them that when such complaints are investigated at all they are investigated by inexperienced or incompetent officials, or politicians who usually whitewash anything where their own party is concerned, and he fears that his treatment will become so much harsher on account of his complaint Then again, little credence is placed in a prisoner's word. Undoubtedly the greater majority of them will tell any kind of a lie if they think it will hurt the officials responsible for holding them. But they do not all do so by any means. A really competent prison investigator, with long experience in dealing with prisoners, will be able to sift their stories and separate the true from the false. Then again the average prisoner has little faith that any abuses to which he calls attention will be remedied, and prisoners are rather inclined to regard with contempt any of their number who may be "green" enough to feel that he may be able to better conditions.

Occasionally however a prisoner will start to write a book on prison reform. I recall one who did named "Sam Jones" He was employed in the library of a prison in the state of Washington. When he made the rounds among the other prisoners to get their orders for books, they "kidded" him unmercifully, saying that above all things they wished to read "Prison Life Made Easy" by Sam Jones. So far as I know, Jones' book never saw the light of day. Possibly he could reform prisons, but he couldn't reform himself, for he had been out but a few months when he was sentenced again.

CHAPTER VIII

THE HEART OF MARYLAND

As compared with the jails, the penitentiaries of the country have during the
past fifteen years made great strides.
There are some of them it is true which
are so old that it is practically impossible
to use the modern and more advanced
methods of administration. But in most
of these an honest effort is being made
to keep them in as good condition as their
age will permit and to apply such
modern methods as are possible in spite
of the handicaps. Once every so often
however, something occurs which shows
that here and there one is still being con-

ducted as most of them were fifty or
seventy-five years ago. Such a one I
found the Maryland Penitentiary, at
Baltimore, to be about two years ago. I
made an investigation of that institution
during the fall of 1920, and ran not only
into a survival of half a century ago, but
also into a virulent case of community
smugness. It is worth while to go into
a few details of this situation as it affords
a typical illustration of what goes on
when bad conditions are revealed.

Among very many other things I found
that assault and battery such as would
have brought long terms to offenders on
the outside were being practiced daily on
the prisoners. This was most often done
by a former deputy warden, a pacific
weakling of some two hundred and
twenty-five pounds; and a guard called
the "Blackjack King" by the prisoners.
These beatings were not done in the heat
of passion, but most of them were deliberately planned, this "Blackjack
King" being summoned to the former

deputy's office on numerous occasions for the sole purpose of beating a prisoner.

The beatings of Federal prisoners which I investigated were all done without cause and under unusually brutal circumstances, two or three officials usually holding the prisoner while one or two pummeled him. In addition, all the Federal prisoners beaten, without exception, were small men, and in one case the victim was a cripple. Concerning the State prisoners, the amount of unrestrained brutality practiced upon them was indicated somewhat at a public hearing held later by Governor Ritchie when the "Blackjack King" casually stated, in response to a question by the Governor, that he could not remember how many prisoners he had "blackjacked" each year in the twenty-five years he had been at the Maryland Penitentiary, because it might have been a hundred a year or it might have been more.

The outstanding feature of the Maryland situation was the matter-of-factness with which all the other prison officials viewed the almost daily outrages perpetrated by the deputy wraden and guards.

The chaplain was practically the only one who denied actual knowledge of these beatings. But since the slightest occurrence in a prison travels like lightning from place to place, and since hundreds of these beatings occurred, this ignorance on his part is very remarkable indeed.

In addition to the criminal assaults practiced on the prisoners, the general conditions surrounding them if not constituting a legal, at least constituted a human and social crime. The food was of a most deadly monotony. There was almost a total lack of air, exercise and recreation. Sick prisoners who were "laid in" for observation were handled with the most benighted stupidity. Prisoners on restricted diet were not looked out for by the physician. Tubercular prisoners were cut off from air by a high blank wall placed around the porch of the tubercular hospital.

159

When these facts with their scandalous details were made public they created a tremendous amount of public interest in conditions at the penitentiary. From the reaction of the community one would think that such a state of affairs was undreamed of. This could easily have been the case, as investigations made from time to time, both by the Prison Board and grand juries, had invariably resulted in "whitewashes." However, one of the local newspapers immediately attacked my findings. Every revelation was denounced as false, I was jeered at and sneered at as a sentimentalist and "sob sister" and the penitentiary conditions praised to the extreme. What was my surprise then to learn a few days later that every brutal practice, every evil condition, and every vicious principle of mal-administration had been made public seven years before by a commission appointed by Governor Goldsborough and headed by a prominent Baltimore attorney, Eugene O. Dunne.

This commission went into great detail and its full findings were printed in book form. But the same newspaper, dedicated ostensibly to the promotion of public welfare, had succeeded so well in throwing a smoke screen of derision and ridicule of the O'Dunne investigators between the penitentiary and the public that the latter was convinced shortly that all was right with the world and with the Maryland Penitentiary in particular and dropped the matter. Hence, your seeming community complacency. Needless to say, the newspaper in question was bound up politically and in other ways with the existing penitentiary administration.

However, these quite usual tactics under the circumstances failed to smother the issue when I made my investigations. I was representing the Federal Government which had power to act independently of the state, at least in regard to Federal prisoners. And it did. The United States Attorney General announced that the Federal prisoners would be re-

moved to another institution, whereupon
Governor Ritchie held a public hearing
at which all of my charges were proved.

Here a curious situation was disclosed.
The Prison Board of the state was composed of two members who had served
for many years, and of a chairman appointed but a short time before. Of the
veterans, one claimed publicly that he
knew and had known for years all about
the beatings, etc. at the penitentiary,
while the other went on record as saying
that he knew absolutely nothing about
what went on, beatings or otherwise.
Now, which is the more responsible in
such a case, the man who knows all or
the man who knows nothing, I have not
yet been able to decide.

After my charges had been proven
publicly, the grand jury indicted the
ex-deputy and three of the guards concerned in the assaults. This was reported
conspicuously and at length in the press.
But in a few weeks a small item appeared
on an inside page stating that these indict-

ments had been "reconsidered." In place of these four officers there was then indicted a prisoner by the name of Bender on the charge of assaulting an officer, the grand jury thus sanctioning the idea that it is a heinous crime for a prisoner to assault an officer, but none whatever for an officer to assault dozens of prisoners. This affair was an outrageous miscarriage of justice; and one which the community should not have tolerated.

The trouble with the Maryland Penitentiary in 1913, in 1920, and during the years in between, was that the officials were interested first, last, and all the time in the quantity of dollars and not in the quality of men they turned out. A warden was judged as being either good or bad according to whether or not he turned in a good surplus to the state at the end of the year. This was the primary reason for some of the most glaring evils in the administration of this institution. To give the prisoners air, exercise and recreation meant taking them from their

163

work, which in turn meant loss of money to the state. To allow the prisoners in the yard for several hours on sunday (a small enough privilege for a man who is earning hundreds of dollars a year for the state) would require the employment of several more guards, which again meant money. To employ a physician and pay him a sufficient salary to enable him to devote his entire time to the work of the institution, and to employ an assistant for the night (at which time the prisoners received medical attention from other prisoners) called for the payment of additional salaries, which once again meant money. To tear down the two hundred-year-old cell houses, which would not make decent kennels for dogs, again meant money. So I found the Maryland Penitentiary complacently tolerated as a monument to the triumph of dollars over men.

And the jails of Maryland! Who can adequately describe their bestiality—their utterly frigid, filthy desolation?

With two or three exceptions the cells are of stone, and in the winter stone cold; there is no light; there is no fresh air, and the atmosphere of decades, poisoned by the exhalations of countless prisoners sick and well, is rendered still more foul by the loathsome night bucket; bathing is usually unknown; bedding is considered plentiful when a mere mattress and a blanket are supplied, and often one or both of these are omitted; there is no segregation of sex, or age, or anything else; there is no exercise, no work, no occupation or diversion of any kind—it is impossible even to see in most places because of the darkness. The only positive qualities that obtain, and these they have in abundance, are dirt, vermin and the execrable fee system of feeding. Life here is indeed not only debased and stripped of every sign of civilization; it is a living death in cold, dark tombs.

The Cecil County jail at Elkton is a stone cavern. There is no cell block, the cells having the outside wall of the jail for their own rear wall. Such light as gets into each cell must filter through a small, obscure pane in a chink about ten inches wide, high up in the wall over the prisoner's head. Though the corridor which runs between the cells is fairly warm, the cells are freezing cold. At one end of this corridor is a pile of rubbish, now two or three feet high, and one of the cells which the sheriff showed me was jammed with torn paper and trash. Just why it should be considered necessary to add to the other vicious features of the jail the conversion of some parts into a dump I do not know. There are no tubs, nor showers, nor toilets. Men or women or children are confined in these cells, each one of which has both a barred and solid door. As the men prisoners, when in the corridor, could easily communicate with the women through the barred door, whenever a woman prisoner arrives both the barred and the solid door are shut upon her and she is left entirely alone in a freezing airless stone vault.

If such a thing as retributive justice actually exists the county commissioners and others responsible for the Kent County jail at Chestertown will some day be convicted of criminal neglect and contributing to juvenile delinquency, and sentenced to imprisonment in this same human hell. It consists of three or four cells fronting on a narrow corridor. There are one or two small windows at the end of the corridor, but none whatever in the cells, and not a ray of light penetrates them. The corridor has one electric light; the cells none, and they are in pitch darkness. The floor of one of the cells is covered with a quarter of an inch of water and filth mixed. There are no cots. The prisoners simply throw a mattress on the floor and themselves on the top of it. In this particular cell they literally sleep on a damp, dank island of filth, the dirty mattress lying in this liquid which surrounds them on all sides. Into this watery rat hole the prisoners arrested in this county go, innocent and guilty alike, the guilty to serve out their sentences or to be transferred to other institutions, the innocent, who are too poor to give bail, to stay three, four or five months awaiting an opportunity to prove their innocence.

In February, 1923, when I last visited this place a young white boy about nine or ten years old was confined with three negro men, one under sentence to the House of Correction, one charged with assault and one with larceny. They were all locked in the small cell-like corridor together, and at this time appeared to be in close conference.

Homo-sexuality and jails go together. The former is the invariable concomitant of the latter. Now consider what a monstrous crime the state commits against this young boy. The state charges him with breaking into a school house. I charge the state with actively conniving to degrade and debase him, to expose him to infectious diseases and to wreck him

168

mentally, morally and physically.

The quarters upstairs for women are similar, except that the floor is not wet. As usual, there are no arrangements at all for bathing and no toilet facilities. The entire place is squalid, crawling with vermin and desolate beyond description.

At the Queen Anne County jail at Centerville I discovered why the authorities throughout the state do not provide bathing facilities for the jail prisoners. I happened to comment on the complete absence at Centerville of any equipment for bathing, whereupon Mr. Seward, the deputy sheriff, explained that it was hardly necessary as none of the prisoners stayed over two or three months.

At Centerville also are the typical— and horrible—dark dungeons of Maryland, with all the other characteristic features.

The Talbot County jail at Easton is nicely whitewashed, but the same dirt, the same unwashed bedding, the same lack of segregation, and the same conservative attitude toward bathing prevail as elsewhere. It was in this jail that the negro, Fountain, murderer, and famed for his successive escapes, was confined. So benighted is the treatment of prisoners in these county jails apt to become that no sooner did Fountain attract attention than the sheriff permitted him to be viewed as a spectacle, and daily allowed the townspeople and visitors indiscriminately to go through the jail for the mere purpose of staring at this prisoner. A proceeding reminiscent of a gathering of cannibals to inspect the white man they are soon to devour.

The Dorchester County jail at Cambridge is practically a repetition of the Talbot County jail.

One would think that the Kent County jail at Chestertown is as bad a sample of a jail as could be found anywhere. But the Wicomico County jail at Salisbury is worse. It consists of four or five stone vaults on the second floor of the sheriff's home. The largest of these is about four-

teen by ten or twelve, and the others ten
by ten or ten by eight. The sheriff's
wife said that sometimes there are so
many prisoners that it is necessary to
crowd sixteen and eighteen men into one
of these chambers. There are no special
quarters for women or children. They
often have women prisoners, however,
the sheriff's wife informed me. The
women are simply put into any of the
vacant cells. Not only are there no bathing facilities, but there is no water at all
on the floor, and the prisoners simply
wallow in filth. There is the usual cold,
dirt, vermin and darkness. There are no
cots. The prisoners sleep on foul mattresses on the floor. Two or three blankets are in each cells and when there are
more prisoners than blankets the excess
just do without, regardless of what the
weather may be. What bitter fights must
must rage at these times it is easy to
imagine.

I thought surely that the county commissioners were lax in their duties, and

had no idea of the conditions in this jail, but learned that on the contrary they make frequent visits to the institution and each time vigorously complain about the expense of keeping up the jail. A situation full of sardonic humor. Once again I suggest a term of imprisonment for the county commissioners for their criminal neglect and indifference, the sentences to specify that they are to be confined in the same place and under the same conditions which they provide for others.

The Baltimore City jail is by far the best in the state, and is really an unusually well-kept institution. Mr. Lee, the jailer, shows what can be done in an institution of this kind. Although it has a very large and constantly fluctuating population, which renders efficient administration more than usually difficult, work is provided for all the sentenced prisoners and the place is a model of cleanliness from top to bottom. Warden Lee has succeeded in keeping it clean, although parts of it are very old and out of date. The kitchen and store rooms are especially well kept. The difference in the spirit of the prisoners is noticeable at once to anyone experienced in visiting such places. Instead of the usual sullen, insolent and defiant attitude, the phlegmatic apathy and the sluggish inertia, there is a spirit of alertness, of contentment, and of interest in getting things done.

It is true that the Baltimore City jail is under the direct supervision of the municipal officials of Baltimore, and the county jails under various county authorities; but surely there must be some phase of state control or authority which could make the institutions within its borders more uniform, and which could remove the startling spectacle of a well-kept jail in its largest city, flanked by the extremes of decay and degeneration just outside its gates.

In the Washington County jail at Hagerstown the cells are full of paper, trash and filth. There are not even mattresses and the prisoners, and both men and women must sleep on the criss-crossed iron slats which make up the bunks. Only one blanket is allowed by the county to each person. This blanket constitutes the sum total of the bedding, covering and protection against cold. There is hot water and one of the employees said that prisoners are compelled to take a bath on arrival. Since, however, the blankets in which they must roll themselves that very night are grimy and smeary beyond description, the effect of this initial cleansing is nullified, and I prefer to leave unvisualized what the condition of the prisoners must be at the end of the customary two or three months.

In construction this jail is perhaps the most modern in Maryland. It has a utility corridor and a toilet and wash basin in each cell. But the toilets and basins, in keeping with the rest of the jail, are extremely dirty, thus illustrating the fact that unless competence, enlightened by a modern point of view, go hand in hand with equipment, real improvement is not possible, as the new equipment is allowed to deteriorate as rapidly as it can.

The Baltimore County jail at Towson, while small, is, like the Baltimore City jail, very well kept. It is the ony really clean small jail I have ever seen in Maryland. It suffers, however, from the usual idleness, and the usual lack of air and exercise.

The principal attraction billed at the Carroll County jail at Westminster is rats. The jail offers many varieties and various sizes. They perform all the usual stunts to the distraction if not to the diversion of the inmates. The jail is a small room separated into four or five cells, the whole of which is so dark and gloomy that in the middle of the day it is impossible to distinguish the features of prisoners two feet away. To achieve this effect of perpetual dusk the few narrow windows are made of thick,

175

corrugated and *frosted* glass. What sheer stupidity ever induced those responsible for the jail's construction to make the windows opaque is more than I can imagine. Instead of trying to let in all the light possible, every effort is made to keep it out.

There are no lamps or electric lights. My last visit to this place was in the middle of the day. But I had to have a prisoner precede me with a candle so that I could get some idea of what the place looked like. There are one or two toilets in a pitch black room off the main room. It had one window, which was stuffed with rags to keep the cold air out. There were several buckets of slops at various places in the room, and I am certain that the entire place has not seen a broom or mop or piece of soap in twenty-five years.

The county allows no mattresses and only one blanket to each prisoner. When the present jailer came there were fifteen prisoners confined and not a single mattress, blanket or other piece of bedding in the place. The prisoners either slept on the hard iron of the cots or on the cement floor. The jailer thereupon took matters in his own hands and bought fifteen mattresses and a like number of blankets, sending the bill to the county authorities. Vermin, it goes without saying, are everywhere.

In this neglected tomb a young man was waiting five months for trial on the charge of forging a small check. The jailer's wife informed me that there was very little evidence against him and that she doubted if he would be convicted, but that, even if he were, she felt sure he would not get more than thirty days in jail. Yet by the time he is tried he will already have served five months not only of time but of apprenticeship in the full horrors of an utterly indecent and demoralized life, in an atmosphere which engenders criminal inclinations and in a workshop which trains in criminal methods.

177

No one can go to the usual county jail in Maryland for a first term without experiencing a tremendous shock. This is followed by a let down of moral calibre which finally results in a complete surrender of all personal dignity and self respect. In the degree of civilization to which we have today attained, the conditions under which these prisoners live, made still more painful by the fee system of exploitation, is no doubt a subtler torture than the kind which prevailed in mediaeval times. After a term in one of the jails in the heart of Maryland, there is no degradation to which a man or woman would feel strange. And this is the crux of the situation with regard to American jails. Men, women, or children are taken by the authorities and are subjected in the name of the state to every debasing influence which can be supplied and exposed to dangers and diseases which may wreck their entire future lives and those with whom they come in contact. They are in the name of the state shown sights and taught things they have never dreamed of. In the name of the state these men, women and children are made accustomed to the lowest of the low and thereafter nothing can be so low that they cannot conceive it, feel it, or do it.

CHAPTER IX.

PERSONNEL — ESCAPES — ADMINISTRATION

Calibre of Officials — Lack of Equipment — Necessary Qualifications—A Unique Situation—Sexual Perverts—Mental Defectives—How the Crucible Shapes the Unformed Official—Escapes—A Leather Ladder and a File Firearms — "Prison Simples" — Wooden Guns — Prison Table Etiquette—"Flying a Kite"—A Message in Cipher —The Rule of Silence—The "Snitch" System—Some Ingenious Escapes—Contraband—Jailers and Wardens—A School of Penology the Remedy—Courses of Study, etc.

One of the great causes of the conditions existing in our jails and prisons today is that in many cases the men selected to conduct such institutions, as well as their subordinates, are entirely untrained for their work. Almost without exception jail officials look upon their offices merely as jobs, which have been given them because they are good Democrats or Republicans, and have worked hard for the party. The average jailer's conception of his duties is simply that he is not to let prisoners escape. Of his obligations and responsibilities concerning the moral and physical welfare of his charges he has not the slightest idea, and in the majority of cases he does not pretend to have. This is true of the largest communities in the United States, as well as the smallest.

I do not believe similar conditions exist in any profession which requires the handling of or association with humans. When we want school teachers we train them for a number of years, as we do physicians and lawyers. Even policemen and detectives undergo a period of training. But in choosing a warden for a penitentiary, or a jailer for a jail, his equipment or experience or any special fitness for the work in hand is usually not considered. It is quite commonplace to see as the heads of such institutions, business men, soldiers and politicians— and these totally unprepared. Like the banker who was appointed warden of a West Virginia institution, these officials are utterly at sea, and usually at a loss not only "what to do next," but what to do first.

181

The heads of such institutions must be men of some education and understanding, and it is absolutely necessary that not only they, but also the rank and file should be trained for their positions. No matter how capable business men, soldiers, politicians, etc., may be in their own fields, it is almost impossible for them to display the same efficiency in the prison world which is entirely different than anything they have even dreamed of. While it may be contended that men have been known to go from one kind of activity to another with success, a similarly successful transposition does not hold good when applied to the prison world, for no other sphere in life affords a parallel to it.

In every other field the business man comes in contact with men who, speaking generally, have the same outlook on life, the same understanding of values and the same system of morals as he himself has. He is thus enabled to estimate them by the very convenient method of asking himself how he would act under like circumstances. But take this man suddenly from his business or trade and thrust him into prison or jail work. He feels as strange as though he was suddenly projected on to Mars. He must conduct, under unnatural conditions, the lives of men and women of two classes with which he had never before had even an indirect contact.

On the one hand he is surrounded by young persons just starting on the downward path and in the formative stages of their careers, to whom a little sympathetic understanding and kindly advice from those in authority may mean the beginning of an honest life. On the other hand he has to deal with the most vicious, resourceful and determined criminals, quick to take advantage of the slightest opportunity to "beat the game." Of the latter class many are abnormal or subnormal. They comprise every shade of degeneracy and vice.

Besides the better known forms of

crime and criminal temperament, the new official has to contend with the whole tribe of sexual perverts. They constitute one of the real problems of every penal institution. Right here/the new guard or warden, though perhaps sophisticated and worldly wise in the ordinary acceptation of those terms, is confronted with a class of persons concerning whose existence he had only the slightest previous knowledge, if indeed he had any at all/ I have seen within the walls of one prison practically every variety of sexual pervert—the masochist, the sadist, the fetichist, the negrophile, the necrophile, the flagellant, and even the narcist, the rarest of all. In addition there is the large body of mental defectives, the moron, high, low and intermediate; the cretin, the mattoid, and in fact every conceivable variety of abnormality or subnormality. Besides these, as aforesaid, there are just the plain dyed-in-the-wool criminals and scoundrels, who would rather go crooked than straight and would kill their own mothers if it would redound in any way to their own advantage.

It is into this seething cauldron that the new official is projected, and the new official is legitimate prey for every scheme and artifice, every deception and trick which may have been old to the criminal classes for countless years, but which are always new to him. The inevitable reaction takes place. At the end of a year or two, after he has found that this vicious class has deceived and imposed upon him, has taken advantage of every trust, has construed every privilege as a right and every liberty as a license, the bewildered and disillusioned official loses sight entirely of the human element and looks upon every man or woman in his charge, whether young or old, convicted or unconvicted, as an utterly hopeless scoundrel, who is not entitled to any more consideration than a beast. He loses sight entirely of the other class, the smaller class, it is true, but nevertheless sufficient in numbers many times over to justify efforts at reclamation. It follows after this as a matter of course that every rule of discipline and every method of administration are designed, not to help the smaller class of which something might possibly be made, but merely to hold in check, for the time being, the more vicious class. Thus by slow evolution the new official comes to feel that his only duty is to see that prisoners do not escape.

But with all this concentration on escapes, I seriously doubt if there is a prison or jail in the world from which prisoners have not escaped. Nor do I believe such a one will ever be built. The reason is plain. Every hour of every day, year in and year out, prisoners in every institution in the world, from the small county jails to the enormous penitentiaries which are practically cities in themselves, are engaged in a never-ending struggle to outwit their keepers. Also in every institution housing more than twenty-five or thirty men there is always one and sometimes many more who are far more clever and intelligent than the jail officials themselves. Living under our jail system of complete idleness, which leaves them nothing whatever to do with their time but to think up schemes to outwit their custodians, it is only natural that escapes should be attempted frequently and that some of them should succeed. The fact that out of the hundreds of escapes attempted only a small number succeed is in itself a tribute to the watchfulness of the prison officials. Their very lives depend on such vigilance, as perhaps 25 per cent of the escapes planned contemplate the murder of some of the keepers to insure their success. It goes without saying, however, that the officers have every advantage. They have bars, bolts, locks and stone walls to help them keep the prisoners from escaping, while the prisoners must find some flaw in this armor or think of some scheme to render it ineffective. And the tricks and schemes and uncanny mechanical skill which the prisoners do use, the courage and resourcefulness which they display, and the ant-like patience with which they execute their plans for a "getaway," would get them far along the road to success if applied in a proper direction. The following incidents will give some idea of what the warden—and particularly the new warden—is "up against" in the matter of escapes.

By far the greater number of escapes are attempted at night after the prisoners are locked in their cells. There are several reasons for this. In the first place, once they are clear of the prison, concealment for the first four or five hours—the most vital in every getaway— is considerably easier than in the day time; if the prison is located in the city there are fewer people on the street; if in the country, the prisoner can, by keeping clear of the roads, avoid people altogether, as no one is then working on the farms. In the second place, the number of officers is reduced to a minimum at night. An institution employing one hundred officers in the daytime will probably not have more than twenty to twenty-five on duty at night.

After a prisoner gets out of his cell, he is far from being free, as he is then faced with the still more difficult task of escaping from the cell house. In practically all prisons, not jails, one or two guards are locked in the cell house with the prisoners at night. This cell house guard has no key and must himself be let out after his tour of duty. Sometimes also there is an armed guard patrolling a high gallery runnnig along the walls of the cell house. This is known as a gun gallery. In properly built prisons there is always a space of from twenty-five to fifty feet left between the top of the cell block and the roof of the building. To escape through the roof this space must be bridged and the trap door in the ceiling opened, or a hole chiseled through.

In the prison I have in mind there are five tiers to the cell block, and a distance of thirty-five feet between the top of the cell block and ceiling proper, where there is a trap door to the roof. Four separate and difficult obstacles to be overcome before the prisoner is even outside. And this is how "Dick" did it.

"Dick" worked in the shoe and harness shop of the penitentiary under the eye of a foreman and a guard on an elevated platform, where it was not easy to walk off with things. Yet he had gradually stolen about two dozen thongs of heavy leather, each eighteen inches long, several dozen small staples and a piece of rope about forty feet in length. To these he added a large hook, which he picked up on the grounds of the institution while some building operations were in progress.

The ends of the thongs of leather he fastened together with a small staple in such a way as to permit them to be opened into a straight line in the manner

190

of a carpenter's rule. The large hook was attached to the last thong and a drawstring ran along the entire length to keep it rigid. Closed it was eighteen inches long, but when unfolded and made rigid it had a length fo about thirty-six feet. When he was not working on this contrivance "Dick" hid it by strapping it flat to his leg beneath his trousers.

During the same period Dick was steadily solving the problem of departing from his cell. For this he used that first aid to the prisoner—the inevitable small saw. He worked on the bars a little every night, carefully stopping at the approach of the "screw" and beginning again the moment he felt secure. The hiding place he chose for his saw was the pipe of his wash bowl, where he secured it to the cross bar by a scrap of twine.

Then one night when all was ready he let himself out of his cell and cautiously climbed to the roof of the highest tier without being detected by the cell house guard. He then unfolded the leather strips, pulled the draw string rigid, and threw the hook over a ledge projecting from a trap door in the roof. Slowly and with infinite caution he climbed up this queer ladder. Just as he was about to succeed his foot slipped. He made a convulsive effort to catch himself, failed, and fell with a startling crash that awakened every prisoner in the place. But almost immediately he began to think again other means to get away and six months later actually succeeded in doing so.

With few exceptions, one of the cardinal rules of the administration of every prison is that no guns are permitted within the walls. In the vast majority of cases only the guards on the walls and in the towers are armed with guns, never those inside who come in direct contact with the prisoners. The possession of one or two guns within the walls upon more than one occasion has enabled prisoners to effect an escape. If the guards carry guns the prisoners, being greatly superior in numbers, can seize them, and, using the officers as shields against the fire of the guards on the walls and in the towers, can quite easily effect an escape.

Several years ago one of the Federal prisons had just such a "getaway." Twenty-six prisoners walked out at this time, although they had but two revolvers. At a signal a group of them in the yard overpowered several guards. Holding the guards before them as shields, they ran through the main building to the front door and pointing their guns at the guard stationed there demanded that he open the door. To have fired at them would have jeopardized the lives of the guards, "the interference." Needless to say, the door was opened and the prisoners marched out They still had to get by an outside tower, however, where an armed guard was stationed. To their surprise, this guard opened fire. They returned it with the stolen guns and the guard dropped dead. Abandoning their human shields, the erstwhile prisoners "beat it" through the gates and scattered.

The worst class among the prisoners are continually making efforts to secure firearms. They cultivate the friendship of prisoners about to be released, particularly those of weak will, and try to enduce them to maneuver firearms or saws to them or to assist them in some way from the outside to escape. The bolder, more determined prisoners usually turn to "prison simples" for this aid.

"Prison simple" is the name given by their comrades to those inmates whose minds, not any too strong to begin with, develop what is known among prison physicians as "prison psychosis." This is a state of mind arising from the mental inactivity and monotony of their daily lives. It is expressed by a growing tendency to invest each tiny circumstance or happening in their constricted sphere with an importance entirely out of proportion to its real value. Prisoners are

194

not alone in this. It is common to all groups of persons who live cramped, monotonous lives. Among prisoners it is a favorite indoor sport to play on the credulity of these simple ones by filling them with all sorts of fantastic, imaginary tales and watching the effect. But it is to these "prison simples," as said, that the wiser heads turn for dupes to assist them to escape.

One Sunday afternoon about two years ago I was sitting on the porch of the deputy warden's home at one of the country's big prisons when a much agitated "outside trusty" came up and whispered that he would like to see us inside the house. We went in and he carefully took from his blouse two enormous revolvers and a box of 100 cartridges, to which was attached a small slip. On the slip was written a little note signed "Success," wishing the intended recipient all the luck in the world. "Old Calamity" (prison slang for deputy warden) was not surprised. It was exactly what he had been expecting for months, and was the very reason that this particular prisoner had been made an "outside trusty." He had been set to watch for some guns to be "planted" on the prison farm, the deputy having known through the prison "underground" that one of his "hard-boiled guys" had been cultivating the friendship of a "simple" whose term would soon expire. The "trusty" who found the guns and turned them in was "doin' it all" as the prisoners say of a "lifer", and had nothing to lose. Several times before he had helped to checkmate similar plots.

A new and original scheme to get hold of a gun was attempted recently in a prison in Kansas. This institution had a "gun gallery" in the cell house. Gun galleries are purposely built high and away from the cell block, so that prisoners cannot get to the armed guards who patrol them. In this institution there was a space of forty feet from the platform running around the cells to the gun gallery on the wall. It would be impossible to imagine a gun inside the cellhouse in a safer position. But the prisoners, to whom everything is vulnerable until proved otherwise, planned to overcome this difficulty by lassoing the guard, dragging him off the gallery and seizing his gun. This could have been accomplished easily, as some of the prisoners were cowboys and thoroughly familar with a rope. However the plot was discovered and led to the building of a grating around the gun gallery to protect the guard from prisoners locked in cells forty feet away.

But the more brainy prisoner is by no means dismayed when he finds his enforced home so "airtight" as to make the smuggling of guns practically impossible. Realizing that the effect of a gun, like beauty, is in the eye of the beholder, he devotes his time to the making of "phony," of dummy guns.

You would never think, to look at the

197

quiet, bespectacled, Murdock that here was a man with the brains to conceive an ingenious escape and the courage and force to lead it. The officials didn't, either, although they are not often fooled by a pleasant exterior. They realize that there are others like the "mildest mannered man who ever scuttled ship or cut a throat." Now, I know Murdock well, and I don't believe he would actually do these things to a ship or a throat, but he could no more help using his brains to concoct schemes than he could help breathing. And when he informed Hewitt, Kating, Grigware, Clarke, Gideon and one other "lifer" whose name I do not recall that he had the "big idea" for a getaway he found willing, not to say eager listeners.

Murdock was employed in the carpenter shop. He worked secretly at odd moments for four months, and at the end of this time he had made several perfect "dummy" revolvers out of ordinary wood, painted black. He carved wooden "bullets" inside the gun chamber and burnished them to look like lead.

A few days later at breakfast in the mess hall Murdock yawned and stretched his arms above his head. With eighteen hundred men present, the fact that one of them yawned and stretched attracted no particular attention. But to every man concerned in the plot it was the most momentous yawn they had ever known. It signified that all was in readiness, and that the first engine that shunted freight into the yard of the institution after that time was the one to be seized. It was customary for the engine to give one whistle after the freight car was uncoupled, as a signal to the guard stationed at the gate to open it to let the engine out. For many years freight cars had been shunted into the yard in this manner to be unloaded.

Each of the men concerned in the plot worked in a different shop. As they started to work after breakfast on this particular morning each carried concealed in his blouse one of the dummy guns with its wooden bullets. There followed two hours of suspense, during which, with every quivering nerve at highest tension, the men waited for the telltale whistle.

At last it came and a simultaneous commotion ensued in each of the shops where the men worked. Gray racing figures bounded past the shop guards like streaks of light and seven determined men were racing to a common point, the cab of the engine. The first to reach the goal was Gideon. He thrust his harmless gun into the engineer's face, who promptly leaped for the ground, closely followed by his fireman. The other prisoners piled into the cab. With a vicious wrench Hewitt pulled the throttle wide open and the engine tore through the open gateway at breakneck speed out into the open country. But they were not yet out of danger. There was a derailing switch built outside the gate for just such an emergency. Deputy Warden Lemon rushed out of his office, built in the center of the prison yard, raced to the switch and threw it over. He was ten seconds too late. The engine passed the switch at thirty miles an hour and picking up speed.

The prison siren began its wailing scream, notifying the country for miles around of the escape and the usual reward for recapture. And of the seven —irony of ironies—Gideon was brought back to the point of an *unloaded* gun in the hands of a neighboring farmer boy, fourteen years lod.

An outstanding feature of this plot was that seven prisoners were planning it together over a period of months, during which time under the "rule of silence" they were neither permitted to talk nor correspond with any other prisoner but their cellmate, and then only at night after being locked in. How, then, did they accomplish their conspiracy? By the prisoner's "wireless" which every man learns in institutions where the rule of silence is in force

One method is to talk into an empty cup while sitting next to each other at the dinner table. Prisoners have developed to an unusual degree the ability to talk through the corners of their mouths without moving their lips. This is the familiar stunt made much of by vaudeville performers when imitating criminals and other denizens of the underworld. In this way one conspirator often manages to talk to another in the yard. Their procedure for making an engagement is the "punch paper" code. This consists of punching pinholes through the words of a newspaper which are needed to make up a message. For instance, if Murdock wanted to talk to Grigware he would punch a pinhole through the words "Stand next to me tomorrow." The paper was passed to Grigware through the prison "underground." He would then hold the paper up to the electric bulb in his cell and pick out the words through which the light showed.

Another of the "wireless" methods is

to communicate by tapping with the fingers when sufficiently close, somewhat on the plan of the Morse code. Sometimes too, prisoners manage to plant notes in various parts of the prison which are to be picked up by the intended receipient. This practice of "shooting" contrabrand notes is known among the prisoners as "flying a kite." They are clever enough to put these notes in code, so that if they should be found by any of the guards they would be meaningless. Such codes are in general use by prisoners everywhere. Just a short time ago, while making a prison investigation, I picked up the following note written in code.

Decoded, this reads: "See Shorty. Get him plant two guns on prison farm at base of oak tree at end of pig pen."

I worked over this cipher message with some of the institution officials for several hours and finally solved the problem by using the word "prison" as a base, feeling certain that it would be employed somewhere in the message.

So many and so effective are the ways devised by prisoners to controvert the rule of silence that prison officials gradually came to recognize its uselessness, and although continued until quite recently it has finally been abandoned.

A prisoner confined in an asylum for the criminal insane in Washington molded a beautiful "gun" out of a piece of kitchen soap, covering it with finely polished tin foil to give it the appearance of silver mounting. Luckily the officers of the institution "disarmed" him before he could carry out his plan to escape. This prisoner had been a tramp, or "blanket stiff," as they are known among the denizens of the underworld. It had probably never occurred to him to look upon soap as other than an offensive weapon. This perhaps may have been the germ of his idea.

The rule of silence, touched upon previously, was not primarily for the purpose of punishing the prisoners and making them feel their degradation. Its purpose was to prevent organization. An old and generally correct theory of prison administration is that the safety of a prison depends upon lack of organization among the prisoners. It was generally thought that organization could be prevented if the prisoner were prohibited from talking. Of course, the prisoners outnumber the officers many times over and if they ever acted in concert they would sweep all before them.

In practice, however, it was not the rule of silence which operated to prevent organization, but certain of the prisoners themselves. In school they would be known by the descriptive "tattle tale." In prisons they are designated "snitches," "snakes" or "stool pigeons." In plain words, they are sneaks of the same kind you meet in everyday life, those who endeavor to "stand in" with their superiors by tattling about others. They are far more numerous in prison than elsewhere, and they are hated by the other prisoners when they are known with a bitterness which is indescibable.

I say "when they are known." The "snitch" is careful to see that he does not become known. When a prisoner tells you he is going to "get" another because he "done the big squeal" you can make up your mind that he feels he has been thoroughly outraged and that the "snitch" had better "keep his eye on his number."

The officers of all penal institutions take every advantage of the "snitch" and of his ability to remain unsuspected. It is this class of prisoner which prevents organization among his fellows, because they never know whom to trust and whom to suspect. A thoroughly detestable kind of person, they have nevetheless prevented many escapes and saved the lives of numberless prison officials. Every prison official has his "stool pigeons," who keep him informed as to what is going on in his institution. And the eagerness with which he uses them is only exceeded by the contempt in which he holds them.

Personally I do not by any means condemn the "snitch" system. On the contrary, I think that as our penal institutions are at present conducted it is absolutely indispensable. I realize that I
lay myself open to the charge of theorists
and moralists that I am upholding the
development of sneaks and hypocrites.
Theoretically it's indefensible. Practically it is not only defensible, it is essential to prevent escapes and protect lives.
But, you say, we don't have to have
"snitches" in everyday life. Of course,
we don't But men in everyday life are
not living unnatural lives under a system
of repression as they are in penal institutions. And where they do you'll have
the "snitch" system on the outside, as
Russia had it under the Czar.

Perhaps I can better illustrate by a
typical incident. A new official had
taken charge. He had had no experience
whatever with prisoners, and was full of
the beautiful theory that you could

handle all of them on an "honor" system, just as you would in college. His first act was to assemble the men in the dining room and tell them that he hated a "snitch" above all things and that the first man who attempted to tell him anything about another prisoner "would be kicked down the stairs" from his office. About two weeks later a prisoner slid up to him in the yard and out of the corner of his mouth conveyed information that one of his fellows had secreted some guns and dynamite in the yard and intended to blow up the place that night and endeavor to effect a wholesale escape. Did he call him a "contemptible 'snitch' "? Did he "kick him down the stairs"? Did he? He did not. He did just what you or I or any one else would do. He accepted the information gratefully and took immediate steps to checkmate the plot. An hour later he had in his office a nice little collection which included ten revolvers, 200 rounds of ammunition, a dozen dynamite sticks and some percussion caps and fuses. Another thing which he had was a firm belief in the use of "snitches."

Very often it appears easier to the prisoners to cut through the walls than to attempt to sever the bars. All kinds of tools have been used for this purpose, and it is not at all unusual for a prisoner to cut through a wall several feet thick with an ordinary tablespoon, a kitchen knife or half a pair of scissors. As this work is slow it is necessary to use every precaution to keep hidden the opening which is being made. The usual method is to stuff back into the opening when work is suspended all the materials which have been dug out and again remove them when an opportunity presents itself. But sometimes the material taken out does not have the proper consistency to hold it into place when put back. One prisoner solved this difficulty by stuffing wet bread into the opening which had been made and rubbing powdered cement and dirt over it to give it the same color as the other portions of the wall.

No space seems too small for a prisoner to crawl through. Years ago jails were constructed with no openings in the walls, except a narrow slit about eight or ten inches wide in the back of each cell, about eight feet from the ground. It was so small that the possibility of ever getting through it was not even considered. One of the jails in Pennsylvania—my recollection is that it is the jail at Sunbury—is so constructed. There had not been an escape through these windows in over fifty years. However, one prisoner did manage to get through. To make himself more slender than he was by nature he dosed himself with purgatives for an extended period. He then greased his body with lard or butter stolen from the kitchen where he worked and after several hours of effort succeeded in squirming through this small opening, a gladder and greasier man.

Once in a while even sewers are used by prisoners to assist them to freedom. The Maryland prison, at Baltimore, had an escape of this kind some time ago. The prisoner who made the escape had a friend who had just been released. Every day after the friend left the prisoner might be seen casting a sidelong glance at a small grating in the corner of the prison yard. A day went by. Then two. Then three. Then one day he saw a small scrap of red rag lodged against the grating, apparently washed there by the rain. But that night while the men were lined up in the yard ready to march in to supper Murphy (which isn't his his name) managed to lose himself for a few minutes. The men went in to supper. Murphy lifted the grating, almost large enough to accommodate a man, squeezed himself in and replaced it after him.

Then began a journey the like of which few men would dare attempt. The drain pipe led into a much larger one, about four feet in diameter, but in which a man going through could not stand erect. It swarmed with enormous rats, was full of sewer gas and filled generally with filth. For half a mile in complete darkness this prisoner crawled and waded, sometimes in water up to his waist, engaging every foot of the way in a constant battle with rats. Every yard seemed harder to pass than the one before. He was just about to give up the struggle when he saw a sickly yellow gleam of light. A last desperate effort brought him to the mouth of the sewer, and there, hidden alongside of it, as his friend has promised, lay a complete outfit of civilian clothing. The change was hurriedly made and Murphy fled, never to return.

And now meet the real hero of the occasion, Mr. Cronin, ex-prisoner, who for no other reason than pure friendship for Murphy, had entered the sewer at its mouth, fought his way up against the current step by step to the grating, where he tied the little piece of red rag as a signal that all was in readiness. Greater love than this hath no man.

This same trick was tried in another prison. There the pipe, however, did not run into a sewer, but just to a corner of the prison farm. "I'll stop that," said the warden. So near the end of the drain he took out twenty-five feet of the large pipe, replacing it with a battery of small ones through which no man could possibly crawl. He figured that the next man who tried to get away would go to all the trouble the first one did and then find further progress barred when liberty was just in sight. Two days later another prisoner took this road to freedom. When he reached the battery of small pipes he was not at all dismayed. He had already provided for that. Taking from under his coat the hammer and chisel which he had brought with him he cut a hole through the top of the large pipe, scraped away a few feet of earth and came headfirst up into the outside world.

Escapes and attempted escapes are not by any means confined to men. Women prisoners do not take kindly to the deprivation of liberty any more than do their brothers. But in proportion to their totals I believe that the number of attempted escapes by men is ten times as many as by women. The reason has always seemed to me that women know their recapture is much easier, particularly if the institution happens to be located outside a city. A woman cannot tramp through the country alone, begging a ride here and there in an automobile, "hopping" freight trains, loafing around railroad yards and doing similar things without exciting a vast amount of inquiry and suspicion. For this reason most of the escapes by women are made from reformatories, where the girls are usually young and inclined to look upon a "getaway" as a lark. In most of the reformatories it is simply a case of walking out, as the girls are allowed ordinarily around the grounds of the institution, which are not always protected by walls. The officials know, as well as the girls, that their recapture is almost certain.

At the reformatory at Bedford, N. Y., there have been frequent escapes. Recently three girls walked away. About an hour or two later they asked a chauffeur to give them a lift. He rode them over strange roads for a while, leading them to believe that he was taking them to New York. Suddenly, after rounding a curve, he stepped on the gas and brought the machine up short directly in front of the institution. He had known all along that the girls were from Bedford and had merely "kidded 'em along." So that was all of that.

A short time ago two women in a prison in Indiana, securing a wire cutter, cut through the heavy metal screen of the window of their room, climbed out to a rainspout just outside the window and slid to the ground. This happened at 3 o'clock in the morning. By 9 they were back in again, each with three years more to do.

I investigated the escape of Robert Fay from the Federal prison in Atlanta. Fay, it will be remembered, is a German who was convicted during the war of placing bombs on American ships. He got away with ease. With another prisoner named Knobloch, his cellmate, he forged a pass in the name of Mr. Bixby, the chief engineer, which permitted them to go out into the yard of the institution. They secured a ladder, some rags and some coils of wire and presented their pass to the guard, stating that they had been sent to clean and fix electric lights in the yard. They spent about fifteen or twenty minutes pretending to fix lights. Then they presented the pass to one of the tower guards, stating that they had been sent to fix the lights on the grounds of the warden's residence, which was further away. This they did so cooly and with such an air of authority that the guard did not telephone into the deputy's office to verify the pass, as he was supposed to do, but permitted them to go out. The pair then graciously spent another fifteen or twenty minutes pretending to fix lights here and there, their labors taking them further and further away from the prison, until, like the Arabs, they silently stole away.

Like many other escapes, this one illustrates that, no matter how secure bars and bolts may be, it is in the last analysis the human element which must ever be recognized. Crooks, like love, laugh at locksmiths.

All prison men said of McG.... that he had "done his bit in every state in the country." This may not have been strictly true, but he had nevertheless a criminal record that indicated a very active life for a man of his years. He was known far and wide as a "bad hombre," consequently when he was taken temporarily from prison across the country to Portland, Ore., to testify in a case in which he was an important witness, the warden called in Y.... and W...., the guards who were to accompany him on the long journey, and impressed upon them the need of caution to see that McG.... did not get away He told them that McG.... had been boasting that they would never get him to Portland and that there was no doubt he would attempt to escape on the way.

Y....had been a guard for more than twenty years, and he informed the warden that he knew prisons and prisoners inside and out, and that there wasn't any prisoner who could escape from him. Two days later the three were on the North Coast Limited going through Idaho. The train had just passed Sand Point when McG....asked to go to the lavatory. Y.... accompanied him and held his foot in the door. McG....suddenly stamped on his foot and as he involuntarily withdrew it slammed and locked the door. Y.... rushed around to the platform, opened the vestibule door and looked out. This did not take a minute

The window to the lavatory was open, but McG.... had disappeared as though the earth had swallowed him. Y.... sprang for the emergency bellrope and stopped the train with a jerk that lifted the passengers out of their seats. As the train came to a stop Y.... and W.... alighted and ran back along the track. There had been a light snow and they figured it would be easy to see where McG.... had alighted and trace him. But there was not the slightest sign of a footstep in the snow, so there was nothing to do but finally board the train again and go on to Portland. A puzzling case, as Dr. Watson would say? Not at all. McG.... had figured that his recapture would be easy if he alighted, so he didn't alight. He merely grab a small rod above the lavatory window on the outside of the train and drew himself up to the roof, where he threw himself flat on his stomach and in this manner rode into Portland, alighting a mile or two from the station when the train slowed down.

He made the entire trip not three yards from his erstwhile custodians.

Hardened as McG.... was he actually wrote a letter to the warden about a week later begging him not to discipline either of these guards as they had both been very vigilant and had used every precaution in guarding him. He assured the warden that he would have escaped from any other guard just as easily, and that both Y.... and W.... had simply been out of luck in being chosen for the trip.

An ingenious escape was made several years ago by a prisoner confined in an insttution on the Pacific Coast. At that time the uniform of stripes was being used. Incidentally, it may be stated that the use of the stripes has caused an endless amount of criticism, and they have now been abolished in practically all the larger institutions of the country. It has been contended, and justly so, that they caused the prisoner needless humilation. But the basic idea of their use was to render his recapture easy if he escaped.

221

In this they failed dismally. Prisoners intending to escape found many ingenious ways of securing civilian clothing. The prisoner in the case I have mentioned could not obtain civilian clothing, so he invented another way out. He contrived to get some dye of the same shade as the dark stripes with which he dyed the white ones. He then stole an overcoat from one of the guards, and this, when the coat was tightly buttoned, made him look like any other civilian, after which escape was easy. He was an "outside trusty" and in his camonflaged stripes, simply walked away.

It is not only against efforts to smuggle in firearms that the prison official must be constantly on the alert, but also against efforts to get in other articles which will assist in effecting escapes. A prisoner receives a magazine from friends on the outside. The mail clerk carefully inspects it, but nothing out of the way is found. He tries to bend it. A sharp snap results. Further search reveals that the entire magazine had been taken apart, a small file placed beyond the stitches between the leaves. It was then completely rebound. Naturally, when it was paged it revealed the leaves only as far as the stitches.

On visiting days prisoners are usually allowed to receive small presents from friends and relatives. At such times a guard is always present, but even the most sophisticated are often fooled. As with drugs, small saws are dropped down a prisoner's blouse by his wife while greeting him with an affectionate hug, and even transferred from her mouth to his while kissing. Apples, oranges and bananas are hollowed so cleverly as almost to defy detection, and saws and other articles to be used in escape placed in them. They have been found in the soles of slippers, combs, brushes and dozens of other articles. Once he has them in his possession the prisoner conceals them in the arm pit or holds them to the sole of the foot with adhesive tape or any other place about his body where it cannot be detected while he is bathing. Of course, many of the jails have no bathing facilities but in the prisons a guard is alway present when the men bathe. There is constant danger of detection in concealing such articles in his cell, as the cells in every well administered institution are searched ("fanned" or "frisked" as the prisoners call it) at frequent and unexpected intervals.

Equally close watch must be kept on prisoners' mail to prevent friends on the outside from arranging to secrete guns or other contraband articles around the grounds or farm of the institution. All sorts of tricks are tried to get secret messages in to prisoners by friends desirous of helping them. It is a daily occurrence in any large prison to detect ciphers, invisible writing which is brought out by water or heat, and similar attempts to communicate secretly. Messages are pasted under the postage stamp on the envelope.

For cool daring the escape of David

Bender from the Maryland "pen" vies with any I know. Because he was considered one of the most desperate prisoners in the institution and had been making repeated efforts to escape for a year or two, every officer in the institution was instructed to keep the closest watch on him and to take no chances whatever. Any attempt to escape was rendered unusually dfficult for him. One day he was quietly working in the shop, watched vigilantly by the shop guard. Like a meteor he suddenly dashed out with the guard in hot pursuit. He ran down the steps, rushed to the wall, grabbed a ladder which despite their precautions he had managed to obtain and secrete for the purpose and in full view of an armed tower guard threw it over the wall, climbed up, flung the ladder over the other side and climbed down. The armed guard, taken apparently by surprise, on which no doubt Bender counted, still made no attempt to shoot him. Bender swiftly jumped aboard a passing motor truck, which the scared driver speeded up at his command, threw his uniform hat and coat into the street to avoid quick detection and passed out of sight while the shop guard was still clamoring for help and the wall guard, with his gun, stood motionless like a painted soldier "against a painted sky."

Inspired by this situation, one of the prisoner wits wrote the following:

Speak kindly to the little "screw"
　Who totes the little gun.
He doesn't know just what to do,
　He thinks it's all in fun.

To shoot a "con" would spoil his day,
　He doesn't think he "oughter,"
The gun with which he likes to play
　Is one that's filled with water.

He doesn't want to be thought rough
　By "gay cat," "stiff" or "faker;"
His gun, it seems, is just a bluff,
　Hence Bender is a "breaker."

In another prison in the middle west the warden was questioning an escaped prisoner who had just been recaptured. After the bird had flown two of the bars of his cell were found to have been severed. Naturally, the warden was curious to know how it had been done, and was particularly anxious to obtain the saw. After a period of sullen silence the prisoner finally declared that he had sawed through the bars of his cell with a piece of yarn taken from his sock, at which the warden became pleasantly sarcastic.

"Sure," he said, "and when that wore out you used a cream puff."

But the prisoner stuck to his story so insistently that the warden, who was somewhat of a "sport," made an agreement with him that he would not take away any of his "copper" for attempting to escape if he would sever a bar in the way he claimed he had. The prisoner went back to the carpenter shop in which he worked, took several pieces of yarn from his sock, dipped them in glue, rolled them through emery powder, allowed the entire mass to dry and harden and sawed through a cell bar in twenty-one hours of actual working time.

Picture the difficulties under which he had originally worked; the perseverence, determination and vigilance that was demanded of him. Each night he would devote a few minutes at a time to sawing, at the same time keeping a hand mirror projecting a few inches out of his cell. This is an old prison trick and enables a prisoner to tell when the "screw" is coming up the runway on which the cells face. The guards wear "sneaks," so their approach cannot be detected. When he saw the guard coming he would discontinue sawing, leap into bed and feign sleep, again resuming his work after the guard had passed. He was not at all discouraged at being recaptured, but calmly announced that he would "git another chanct."

The above illustrations give some idea of what the custodian of a penal institution has to reckon with in the matter of escapes. To combat successfully the ingenuity of prisoner brains involves difficulties and sometimes novel complications. However, prevention of escapes is largely a matter of routine and it is the variation where special steps and precautions must be taken. In properly managed institutions all due care is taken to see that the prisoners do not escape while at the same time the other features of prisoner life are not neglected. It is absurd for a warden or jailer to feel that his only duty is to prevent escapes, as that should occupy only a small fraction of his time and attention. Of course, if the warden or jailer is to begin with of a coarse, illiterate type, with the widely prevalent attitude that anything is good enough for a prisoner, he is naturally unable to do more than see that men and women are simply confined to the place where they are put. Or if the jailer or warden is a man of some education and perception— the banker, politician, soldier or newspaper man—but has no knowledge and experience of the management of prisons and prisoners he whirls around the vortex

229

of claims and counter claims, rumors, stories and suspicious until, exhausted, he clutches at and clings to the one obvious responsibility of preventing escapes, while almost all other matters are administered along the lines of least resistance. Only a man of competent calibre to begin with enlightened with adequate penal training and experience, can, except in rare cases, step into a jail or prison and conduct it so as to serve the best interests of both the prisoners and the public. It is not enough even for a man to go into a jail or a prison and maintain it at the level previously reached, for most of the jails and many prisons in the United States are at a very low level indeed and need men to do constructive work—men who can improve matters all along the line. As matters stand at present, one is apt to find the warden of a penitentiary a desirable man; but the jails usually have only unintelligent, densely ignorant and illiterate men in charge.

There should be a school of penology in the United States, and men who wish to follow jail and prison work as a career should attend it, just as those who are to become doctors and lawyers attend medical and law schools. As I have before stated, there is no other field of work that parallels it, and no man, regardless of how capable he may be along other lines, can bring to jail or prison work the equipment necessary to make such institutions laboratories for the scientific study of those who have run afoul of the law, instead of the crucibles of crime which they are at present. Courses should include the study of defectives and delinquents, methods of punishment and restraint, purchase of food supplies, mass feeding, detection of malingering, treatment of narcotic addicts, general study of identification systems, keeping of prison records, different systems of prison labor and the merits and defects of each, compensation systems for prisoners, athletics and recreation, health

231

and sanitation, general business administration, and so on. They should be learned by practical experience, as well as by study. For this no doubt a plan can be worked out whereby young men and women who have completed a certain term of study may spend some time in various institutions, just as our young medical graduates become internes in hospitals for certain periods before going into independent practice. Such a centre of learning would not only turn out men and women really equipped to serve federal, state and municipal governments, but would also stimulate a deeper study of penological and criminological problems. Although the body of men in the United States equipped practically to instruct in these sciences is small, yet there are enough to organize and provide a staff for such a school. And such a man as Dean Kirchwey, who combines both the equipment of the school executive and the penologist, is eminently fitted to help found and carry on such an institution.

232

CHAPTER X

YEARS OF HORROR

Nebraska Jails—Omaha's Swift Deterioration—A Subject for American Women—A Century and a Half at Charleston—How White Women are Treated—Colored Women—Pest Holes of South Carolina—Twenty-eight Instances — "Wiggle Tails" — Michigan's Leadership — Detroit—Chicago Jail a Synonym for Everything Vicious —Demoralizing Idleness—From Richmond to the Border Strip.

It would scarcely seem necessary to continue my recital of the jail conditions in this country, but I do not want the slightest feeling to exist that I may have picked out a few high spots in order to make a case. What I do want is to bring home the fact that, with comparatively few exceptions, such conditions as I have described are universal, and that they exist in every part of the United States from the Atlantic to the Pacific and from the Great Lakes to the Gulf.

Occasionally—very occasionally—an attempt may be made to put a jail into a clean or habitable condition. If such an attempt has been made since my last visit to a place—and it goes without saying that I cannot visit the entire country simultaneously—we can only be glad of this change while realizing that it does not alter the general case in the least. And if one or two particular spots should be cleaned up the week before or the day before this is published, it would neither alter the fact of their years and years of horror, nor alleviate but a trifle the national situation. Bear in mind that to one place here and there which may occasionally receive attention, or which officials may point out as having been altered since I began writing this book, there are a hundred degenerating still further day by day.

There is Nebraska. Until several years ago the Douglas County jail at Omaha was about on a par with the one that existed so long at Peoria. Then they built a fine new one on the upper floor of the courthouse. I visited it about two years

234

after it was completed and found that already it was dirty, ill kept and beginning to show the results of the usual indifference.

Of most of the others in Nebraska the less said the better. Many of them are in the basements of the courthouses, and since the courthouses themselves are very often filthy, the condition of the jails can readily be imagined. As late as 1920 only 36, or considerably less than one-half, had any separate accommodations for juvenile prisoners. Here, women voters of America, is a subject crying for your attention!

Then there is South Carolina. The jail building at Charleston is about one hundred and fifty years old. It outlived its usefulness a hundred years ago and has been gradually getting more unfit since that time, until now no farmer who values his stock, would use it as a barn. During the war, in August 1918, I was sent to Charleston to endeavor to secure accommodations for a large number of women who had been arrested under one of the laws passed during the war designed to protect the health of soldiers. I conferred with a surgeon of the Public Health Service. We found the conditions in the jail to be appalling and at the request of Judge Smith of the United States district court submitted a report to him, which he subsequently gave to the newspapers. This report appeared verbatim in the Charleston News and Courier of August 29, 1918; I am giving it below in full.

Charleston, S. C., August 24, 1918.

Hon. H. A. M. Smith,
United States District Judge,
Charleston, S. C.

Sir:—

Pursuant to your request that we advise you concerning conditions existing In the Charleston County Jail, at Charleston, S. C., we wish to inform you that we visited that institution this morning and made a complete inspection of every portion of it. We submit the following:

As you appeared to be particularly interested in the quarters provided for women, both white and colored, we paid particular attention to that feature. The white women are confined in one large room on the second floor. This room has absolutely no facilities whatever for their comfort and convenience. There is no toilet nor basin in which the women can wash. In fact, there is no plumbing of any kind. The jailer has been compelled to purchase a small galvanized iron tub, similar to a wash tub, in which the women wash. The water, of course, has to be carried in. In the hall outside of this room there is an iron basin which is available for the use of the women, but this cannot be used at night as they are all locked in. They have no toilet facilities whatsoever, and are compelled to use buckets for their personal comfort. These buckets are kept in the room with them all night and are emptied in the morning. The insanitary features of such a condition and the possibilities of spreading disease are too obvious to require further comment.

The room is poorly lighted and ventilated. The room has four or five windows which are not more than sixteen inches wide, and these are heavily barred. There is no matron, and the jailer before he can enter the room, is compelled to knock upon the door in order that the women may be properly clothed upon his entrance. In short, so far as the quarters for white women are concerned, the conditions existing are primitive and barbarous in the extreme, and reflect a lack of interest and understanding of the problem at hand among those who should be interested, that is, to say the least, discouraging.

The conditions existing with regard to the white women apply with almost equal force to the colored. It is true that, so far as their place of detention is concerned, they are somewhat better provided for, but the sanitary features show little if any improvement. The cells have no toilets and during the night buckets are used for the personal comfort of the inmates. During the day they are allowed out in a small corridor between the cells, which gives them access to a toilet in the end of the corridor. They also have acess to a so-called bath, which consists of a small iron tub, in which clothing is washed. One of the most astounding features is that the institution has no hot water whatever, either winter or summer. Under such conditions, of course, it is impossible to enforce rules of regular bathing. To obtain hot water for washing clothing the jailer is compelled to heat it in a large basin over an open fire in the yard. The jail has absolutely no laundry facilities.

The cell blocks for white and colored men are practically similar to that in which the colored women are confined, and the jailer is hampered by the same archaic plumbing arrangements. The toilet in the cell block used for the colored men leaks badly and despite every effort to keep it clean has a very bad odor. The floors have in some places rotted through and the jailer was compelled to put in a coating of cement to avoid seepage to the floor below. The jail is so old that in some places the bars have corroded and in one place at least hang by a rather slender thread. There are two shower baths in the basement, where the white males and the entire chain gang bathe. One of the spigots leaks here and has leaked for several months, and notwithstanding the fact the jailer made repeated efforts to have it fixed no attention has been paid to it.

In a word it might be stated that the generally insanitary conditions existing are due to a combination of age and apparently absolute neglect. It is desired to state that not one bit of this neglect can be charged to Mr. Bennett. He is making every effort with the facilities at hand to keep the place clean and in this he has succeeded remarkably well. Not a criticism can be offered concerning its condition of cleanliness. Mr. Bennett has modern ideas and has made it a point to visit modern institutions outside the State. He has made repeated efforts to have these ideas carried out, but apparently has met with very little success. He is an intelligent man and

238

far superior in every way to the average jailer.

In conclusion we wish to state that we do not consider this institution a proper place in which to confine diseased female Federal prisoners. There is ample room at the institution, by the expenditure of several thousand dollars, to provide good facilities for all prisoners, male and female, and both State and Federal. The institution has a splendid yard which the jailer has in good condition.

We shall be glad to give you such further information as you desire.

Respectfully,

Jos. F. Fishman,
Inspector of Prsions, U. S. Dept of Justice.

Charles V. Akin,
P. A. Surgeon, U. S. P. H. S.
Dept. Venereal Disease Control, S. C.
State Board of Health.

This publicity started such a furore that the state was compelled to take action, and within the last year improvements have been begun.

My first visit to many of the jails in South Carolina was made fifteen or sixteen years ago. Although I have visited these jails many times since and have, I suppose, grown somewhat callous from constant inspections, never will I forget the impression made upon me by that first visit.

239

The jails of thirty-five of the forty-four counties of the State would be abandoned as living quarters by the most tolerant pig. Some of them are a hundred years old, others not quite so ancient. But old or new, with the few exceptions mentioned, they are reeking holes of pestilence. To describe them is to give a monotonous repetition of rotten plumbing, horrible overcrowding, damp, dark, and indescribably dirty caverns, and other conditions the description of which are not printable, all bepeaking a callous and brutal disregard of the most elementary rules of hygiene and sanitation.

Far better, however, than my own general picture of the situation in most of the South Carolina jails, are the terse but vivid portrayals given by their own State Board of Public Welfare in its most recent report.

Abbeville County: The cells are dark and poorly ventilated. The prisoners' quarters have only one bath tub and one toilet. Each cell consequently has to have a refuse bucket as well as a bucket of drinking water, both of them constantly exposed to flies, since the upper floors of the building are not screened.

Aiken County: Badly in need of repairs. The roof leaks. In rainy weather the water pours down into the jail in torrents. Plumbing in poor shape, bath tubs useless, and can only be flushed with difficulty.

Bamberg County: Sewage not properly disposed of. Soil buckets emptied in a hole about 75 yards from the building, but no dirt thrown on it. Flies swarming around.

Beaufort County: Food lacking in variety and wholesomeness. Floor and bedding dirty.

Calhoun County: Lack of facilities results in all the prisoners being herded into one room—*men, women and children.*

Chester County: Scraps of food lying around. Drain pipes from combination drinking fountains and lavatories stopped up with refuse. Bedding and jail dirty.

Cherokee County: Dirty. Dog sleeping on extra pile of blankets. Insufficient food.

Chesterfield: Panes of glass out of windows. Jail improperly heated.

Clarendon County: Cell block needed thorough cleaning, scraps of decaying food lying around. Improperly heated.

Colleton County: Plumbing in deplorable condition. Pipes leak so badly water can be turned on only once a day, when a supply must be caught for drinking, laundering, cooking, bathing, and for flushing the sewerage system. Dirty, no bathing rules, and generally unfit.

Darlington County: Heating arrangements inadequate. Cells dark.

241

Dillon County: In deplorable condition. Defective plumbing. Lower floor of jail had recently been covered with several inches of water. *Jailer's family stated that at this time a negro convict died in the jail of influenza, and the water under his cot was over an inch deep on the night of his death.*

Remember that I have given only a portion of the description. That they are all inexcusably filthy goes without saying. Now, just a few more:

Fairfield County: Floor cannot be scoured because water runs through cracks into sheriff's home below. Building fire trap. Bedding dirty.

Georgetown County: Violently insane man confined in same cell block with another prisoner. Hole in ceiling and roof so that in rainy season the water pours into the building.

Greenwood County: Bath tub for negroes out of commission, and galvanized tubs used instead. Drain pipe of tub for white prisoners clogged so that the water must be emptied by dipping most of the dirty water from it with a pail. Toilets almost beyond use from lack of repairs, and one of them leaking badly.

Kershaw County: Bath tub filled with dirty water and "wiggle-tails." Insufficient food.

Now, I do not now exactly what a "wiggle-tail" is. Previously to reading this I had supposed, in my ignorance, that I had seen every kind of jail vermin.

242

But I presume there are so many varieties that, like the words in the dictionary, no man could possibly learn them all.

Lancaster County: Cells veritable wooden dungeons, with no windows, the only light and air coming through small heavily barred doors. *Even with the cell door wide open the cell is so dark that an inmate cannot see the ceiling clearly enough to tell of what material it is built.* Not one ray of sunlight ever penetrates this house of darkness that is so much better adapted for the habitation of bats and owls than of human beings.

Laurens County: Living conditions extremely unsatisfactory. Toilets out of order and fill building with bad odors. Heating so unsatisfactory that colored men sleep on floor in order to be near stove. Bath tubs useless from lack of repairs. Supply of blankets so scanty that none can be spared during the cold months for the laundry. Men, both white and colored, sleeping under covering that is so soiled that it is positively filthy. Whole building dark and dirty.

Lexington County: Sanitary arrangements miserable. No hot water for bathing. *No stove or other heating facilities at all.* Prisoners suffering with cold so that they used tin tub for stove by filling it with chips and trash. Smoke filled room. But in addition to no heating facilities, *several of the window panes were broken.*

Marion County: Bedding unsatisfactory and generally filthy. Men sleep on pallets on the floor.

And then the board adds "Jailer God-bold is to be commended for his desire

243

to take good care of the prisoners and for his interest in the jail." To use the current slang: Are they trying to "kid" somebody?

> Marlboro County: The building has only two compartments, making it almost impossible to separate properly the prisoners according to *sex*, race and age.

And with slight variations the same criticisms of Oconee, Orangeburg, Richland, Spartanburg, Union, Williamsburg and York Counties.

Is every state so backward in the handling of its prisoners? Almost every one; yet there are brighter spots here and there. Michigan is one of the latter. She affords a really encouraging illustration of what a state can do to remedy conditions in penal institutions. Michigan, like a very few other states in the union, has a law under which the State Board of Charities and Corrections can condemn and close institutions which are unfit, after first giving the offending county an opportunity to make necessary improvements. This board can even institute mandamus proceedings to compel the county to take action. And it is instructive to note that our oft-mentioned community indifference is such here that the Board has more than once been compelled to resort to the courts to force certain counties to remedy conditions which had been repeatedly brought to the attention of the county authorities. Michigan also makes a particular effort to separate the juvenile from the older offenders.

This Board is doing a spendid work, and the law empowering it is a step in the right direction. But even so, do not think that the jails of Michigan are all models, because, notwithstanding the fact that this Board has been in existence many years, many of the jails are still dirty, out of date, and unsanitary, with no proper facilities for the temporary detention of the insane. The jail at Detroit, for instance, due to the city's phenomenal growth, has been greatly overcrowded for a long time. Several years ago it was condemned by the Michigan State Board but no new jail has as yet been built.

In spite of these variations, Michigan is indeed to be congratulated. It has "seen the light" far in advance of the great majority of the other states in the Union and appears to be making a determined and conscientious effort to give its unfortunates at least an opportunity to live in decent, habitable quarters while they are confined. So far so good. As will be explained later on, decent physical conditions are only ten per cent. of the jail problem. The great curse is idleness. This curse Michigan has not lifted so far. Here is a great chance for national leadership for any State in America, because such idleness in the jails is country-wide. It is not too much perhaps, to hope that Michigan, striding ahead in some other jail matters will be the standard bearer in this.

The Cook County Jail at Chicago is

a synonym for everything that is vicious in our jail system. But the one bad feature that, above all others, forces itself upon the attention, is that of idleness, not because it is different from that existing in other jails, but because, due to the large jail population, it is so accentuated. One look at the corridors during the day time when all the prisoners are out will bring home to you with greater force than volumes of writing just what the idleness of our jails means. I have visited the jail at Chicago on numerous occasions, and each time felt more keenly the appalling evil of this stupid, wasteful and demoralizing idleness. Chicago is by all odds the toughest city in the United States, and there are always several hundred prisoners in this institution. With the exception of a few who work in the kitchen and around the jail, no prisoner does one stroke of work from the day he is received until he leaves. At a conservative estimate the value of the labor here wasted is between

247

a half million and a million dollars a year. But the economic loss through the mental, moral and physical stagnation of the prisoners cannot be counted in dollars. It is incalculable. To look into these corridors and see the hundreds of well set-up and able bodied men lolling around doing nothing except becoming more proficient in crime is enough to make one despair of any solution of the criminal problem while idleness continues.

The jails of Virginia almost without exception from Richmond to "the border stip that turns off into the west," and from Winchester all the way to North Carolina, are typical southern institutions. That is to say, the buildings are generally a little more ancient and wretched than in other sections of the country; the interiors more gloomy and squalid; the cells more unkempt and malodorous; the vermin more prolific, and the personnel more ignorant, indifferent and lazy. I do not know of any

248

high lights in the picture of Virginia, but can say in passing that the Henrico County jail at Richmond and the city jail at Newport News cast even darker shadows than the rest. Concerning the whipping of women in the Virginia Pententiary at Richmond and the lack of decent accommodations for them, I have already spoken in chapter five.

CHAPTER XI.

SPECIFIC REMEDIES

Workshop of Crimes——-Dirt——-Showers — Compulsory Bathing—Fumigation—Clothes—Eating in Cells — Overcrowding—Hygiene—Infectious Diseases—Syphilis—Tuberculosis — Prison Doctors — Drug Addicts — Narcotic Cures—Segregation of Juveniles, Sexes and Unconvicted —Unnecessary Delays—Exercise and Recreation—"Pampering" Prisoners—Reading Matter—"Kangaroo Courts" —Duty of the Judge—Fee System of Feeding—The Curse of Idleness—How It May Be Eliminated—"Judicial Districts"—Farming—Compulsory Work Law—State Jails— Prisoners' Compensation — Inspection — Federal Jails — Federal Responsibility.

I do not see anything to be gained by continuing a recital of criminal-breeding conditions in the jails of the United States. All that has been said concerning jails here and there, in Louisiana, Arizona and Kentucky, in Virginia, Arkansas and Illinois, in Ohio, Washington and Florida, in Indiana, Missouri and Nebraska, in Texas, Pennsylvania and Alabama, in Maryland and West Virginia and Kansas, can be said with slight variations concerning jails in practically all other states in the Union. Simply change the name of the place and nine chances out of ten you will know enough from what you have read to describe its jail without even going to see it.

And what is accomplished by such a state of affairs, Are criminals corrected? Crimes made less frequent? No. The only results of the ostrich-like stupidity with which jails in this country are conducted are the conversion of smooth-reading sentences into outrageous injustices and the development of criminal material with its attending increase of dangers to the community.

As they stand at present, the jails of the United States, generally speaking, are giant crucibles of crime. Into them are thrown helter-skelter the old, the young, the guilty, the innocent, the diseased, the healthy, the hardened and the susceptible, there to be mixed with the further ingredients of filth, vermin, cold, darkness, stagnant air, overcrowding and bad plumbing and all brought to a boil

251

by the fires of complete idleness. Only the strongest material can resist such fusion.

So it comes that the penitentiaries of the country, where those convicted of graver offenses are sent, may be regarded somewhat as the showrooms of crime, while the jails afford ample workshop facilities. For it must never be forgotten that every accused person, except those able to give bail at once, goes to jail and goes there first. To one person in the penitentiaries there are a hundred in the jails. Therefore if we are to reduce the number of criminals and check the tremendous social and economic loss due to crime we must put the jail on a sane and sensible basis.

First of all, they should be kept clean. If there is any excuse at all for other existing evils, there cannot be a shadow of justification for the filth and vermin which seem to go hand in hand with our jails. When a jailer tries to tell you that it is "impossible" to keep a jail clean, it usually means that he is either too lazy or too indifferent to try. The surest proof that jails can be kept clean is that a few of them are actually maintained in spotless condition. There is no mystery about it, no secret alchemy which some jailers practice, no trick to which they are privy which the other man cannot hope to learn. They are kept clean in exactly the same way as one's own home is kept clean—by the liberal use of soap and water, mixed with a little care, a dash of pride and a pinch of industry. Only the jailer's problem is easier than the housewife's, as he can have any amount of assistance.

Undoubtedly if they are allowed to go uncleaned for months on end, and even years, as they are at present, they become so thoroughly saturated that they never can be made thoroughly clean again. If a community, either for this reason or any other such as lack of facilities for proper light and air, finds its jails unfit there is only one thing to do, that is to build a new one, and start fresh. It is a radical remedy, but the only one.

Every jail should have a sufficient number of shower baths— not tubs—and a sufficient amount of hot water at all times. It is a monstrous injustice to compel a large number of prisoners to use one tub for both washing clothes and bathing purposes. It is equally unjust to expect them to use cold water for bathing purposes in the middle of the winter. Many persons are physically unable to take a cold bath at any time. And the use of one tub is exceedingly bad even if there be plenty of hot water and it is not used for laundry purposes. For this often brings about the situation previously depicted in this book, when Mrs. O'Hare under threat of punishment was compelled to bathe in the same tub immediately after a woman in the last stages of syphilis.

Every prisoner should be compelled to take a bath immediately upon his arrival and at regular intervals of at least once a week thereafter. Not five percent of the jails of the country have compulsory bathing rules.

If the prisoner is found to have vermin he should be at once separated from the others until he is thoroughly clean. His clothes should be thoroughly fumigated and, if in good condition, again given to him to wear. If not, he should be furnished with an outfit.

Under the present system jails, as a general rule, furnish no clothing at all to the prisoners, and in many instances prisoners suffer greatly from the cold. If a prisoner sentenced for a year has only the most meagre and ragged clothing on his back when he arrives, that is what he must live in until he gets out. Sometimes, indeed, prisoners have such little clothing that they cannot be seen in public and the jailer is compelled to get them some clothing before they can be taken to court for trial. In the jail at Dallas, Texas, now one of the best in the country, prisoners are given a neat uniform of some cheap material.

One practice which tends to make and keep jails insanitary is that of feeding prisoners in their cells, instead of allowing them to sit at a table in the corridor. In possibly ninety-five per cent of the jails in the country a pan of food is passed through the bars of the cell to them in exactly the same way as the animals in the zoo are fed. Very often the prisoner does not eat all the food but allows some of it to remain in his cell for several hours. If he does eat it all the greasy dish often remains for a long time. In either case roaches, mice and rats are attracted, and come to look upon the place as a feeding quarter which never fails them.

Of course it goes without saying that the overcrowding prevalent in so many jails should be immediately discontinued and every prisoner allowed an amount of cubic air space which physicians hold necesary to health. This is now the exception instead of the rule. And that the heating should be sufficient and the plumbing modern and in good repair are too obvious to require comment. Leaky plumbing and the foul odors which accompany it are certainly not conducive to health under the best circumstances, but when you couple them with improper ventilation you provide indeed a good foothold for all kinds of disease.

The most elementary considerations of humanity would seem to call for the complete segregation of all prisoners suffering with infectious and contagious diseases. But, as must be recognized by now, "considerations of humanity" have had no place in our jails. Every prisoner upon arrival should be thoroughly examined by a competent physician. If found to be suffering with a communicable disease he should be kept away from the other prisoners until he is well, meantime of course being given proper treatment. Every jail should have a hospital room for this purpose. Not one in fifty has any hospital facilities now.

It is not only inexcusable to confine with others those who are suffering with communicable diseases; it is criminal. If a prisoner should die from a disease contracted in this way the State is just as guilty of his murder as if it had deliberately inoculated him with the germs. At a conservative estimate I should say that in 3,000 of the 3,500 jails in this country, no effort whatever is made to ascertain if a prisoner is diseased upon his arrival, nor to segregate him if it should be known that he is suffering with a contagious ailment. I have already spoken of one jail where a prisoner in the last stages of syphilis whose mouth and throat were a mass of sores, was drinking from the same glass, using the same toilet and bedding as the other prisoners, and being treated generally as though there were nothing in the world the matter with him. This is by no means unusual. There are many hundreds like it. A very large percentage of jail prisoners have syphilis in an infectious stage. No attempt whatever is made to segregate them, to feed them separately, clean their dishes separately, or in any way to treat them in accordance with the demands and dangers of their diseases.

As the jails are kept at present they are fertile soil for the growth and spread of any disease which thrives especially in filth and insufficient light and air.

A large number of prisoners have tuberculosis, the only known cure for which is plenty of light and air and wholesome diet of milk, eggs, and foods of that kind. The latter cost money, the usual excuse which the counties give for doing nothing. But light and air do not, and the tubercular prisoner do not even get these. They are not even given sputum cups, the most elementary precaution against the spread of this disease. They spit on the floor as do other prisoners thus giving the germs plenty of chance to be breathed in by the others. Those who have gonorrhea and other infectious venereal diseases, use the same toilets as the others, the same drinking glasses and the same bedding, all of which were used hundreds of times before them and will be used just as often after they leave by both healthy and diseased men and women. This includes those awaiting trial, many of whom will never be convicted, as well as those who will eventually be sentenced.

Physicians who attend jail prisoners should make a study of the ailments usual among them. As I have heretofore stated, very few such physicians have even an elementary knowledge of the treatment of narcotic addicts. Their bungling in such cases causes an appalling amount of the most frightful torture, and torture too that is easily preventable. A large percentage of the men confined in jails are narcotic addicts. While I am writing this, I read in one of the New York papers about the arrest at one time of several hundred of these unfortunates charged with violating the Narcotic Act. In a later issue the paper states that one has already died and three collapsed when their drugs were suddenly taken from them, a not at all unusual result unless prompt compensatory treatment is given.

The Special Deputy Police Commissioner of New York in charge of these cases, Dr. Carleton Simon, expresses the opinion that these addicts should be sent to hospitals instead of to jails. But this involves extra guarding and is generally cumbersome and inconvenient. The real solution is to send them to jail where they can be safely held without extra trouble and expense, and have a jail physician who understands how to treat them so as to break them of the habit in a minimum time and with the least suffering.

The treatment and cure of narcotic addicts, even those taking as high as sixty grains of morphine a day, is not at all a difficult matter, and I know of at least two prison physicians in this country who cure hundreds every year, turning them out of the hospital with systematic regularity in from five to eight days.

These are really cures and not temporary lulls in the habit. It is true that many prisoners resume the habit later, but this is due not to a recurrence of the craving, but to a repetition of the original influence of bad associations or some kindred reason. The ability to stay cured is a matter of the individual's own stamina. That subsequent relapses into the habit after these cures is not due to the sudden reappearance of desire is proven by the fact that, after prisoners are once cured, they often remain in prison for many years during which time, by their own admissions, they have absolutely no craving for narcotics.

Segregation, however, should not be confined to the sick. Juveniles of both sexes should, of course, be separated entirely from the older prisoners. It is not enough to confine them in separate cells. They should be in a separate section or wing entirely out of sight and hearing of the older prisoners. What is virtuously called segregation of juveniles in some jails is in reality not segregation at all, but merely separation by a partition.

Every jail should have a matron to care for its women prisoners and should of course have absolute separation of the sexes. The male jailer should only be admitted into the women's quarters with the permission and in the presence of the matron, after the latter has assured herself the women are all fully clothed. It goes without saying that the younger girls should be segregated from the women as the younger boys from the men.

While an attempt is made occasionally here and there at one or more of the forms of segregation mentioned above, one whole important phase of the matter is entirely overlooked practically everywhere. This is the segregation of those awaiting trial from the convicted. The gross injustice to those subsequently proven innocent of herding them in with the guilty is just one of the many outrages which the State perpetrates upon

263

citizens from whom it expects at all times the most upright conduct. More criminal than many of the persons it imprisons is the state which tolerates such practices.

Another unnecessary injury inflicted upon the untried is the practice of compelling them to remain in jail for long periods of time awaiting trial. It is not at all unusual to allow them to remain in jail for one, two, three and four months and sometimes much longer. During the war I came across several cases in which prisoners had been in jail awaiting trial for more than one year. During the summer months many of the courts of the country are in recess, so that a prisoner who is arrested in June, although ready and willing to go to trial, may be compelled to remain until the court reconvenes some time in September or October. This applies to prisoners who intend to plead guilty, as well as to those who intend to stand trial. This state of affairs, however, is by no means peculiar to the summer. In thousands of cases prisoners are held awaiting trial for a long period when the courts are in session.

Here as elsewhere of course the man with money has a tremendous advantage, as he can give bail. But those who cannot simply languish in jail until it suits the pleasure of the officials to try them. Of course, the prosecuting officers cannot try every case at once. Each case requires some preparation, and this requires time. But taking all these facts into consideration I know that, even at a very conservative estimate, the time prisoners spend in jail awaiting trial could be shortened from one-half to two-thirds if the officials honestly made every effort to try them at as early a date as possible.

Many judges will tell you that, when imposing sentence, they always take into consideration the time a man spends in jail awaiting trial. Well and good as to those convicted. But how about those acquitted? And when you add to this evil those which I have already related,

265

you will begin to have some slight idea of the injustice with which many prisoners in jail are treated. It would be bad enough to deprive an innocent man of his liberty for a few hours even under the best surroundings. It is infinitely worse to confine him months longer than is necessary under the very vilest surroundings such as exist in most of our jails.

It is an outrageous injustice to the prisoners for courts to recess during the entire summer. If the judge who works through the winter must have a vacation for several months, someone should be appointed to hold court during that time. If all the physicians in a hospital should suddenly quit at the approach of summer, to resume their duties in the fall, and no substitutes provided meanwhile for the suffering patients, an outraged public would demand an immediate change. This is not worse than keeping a man confined for several months who may afterwards be acquitted. But the man in jail is an under dog among under dogs, and our penal system does its best to keep him under.

The prisoners should be given some exercise daily and some kind of recreation at least once a week. These are not luxuries; they are necessities. They help to keep up to some extent the physical and mental health of the prisoners, and provide a safety valve for animal spirits which everyone requires. In the majority of the larger penitentiaries prisoners engage weekly—usually on Saturday afternoons—in athletics of various kinds, such as baseball, handball, and even boxing. But with very few exceptions none of the jails of the United States give the prisoners any exercise whatsoever, whether they are confined for a day or a year. The result is that the prisoners become flabby and sluggish, while the amount of constipation among them is astonishing. Every jail should have a yard and prisoners should be turned out for exercise for at least an hour or two each day.

As to recreation, the prisoners can be given inexpensive indoor amusements at least once a week. Motion pictures can be shown, and I have always found actors and actresses willing to give free performances in the local penal institutions at any time they are asked. Some of the very best performers appear in such places, and they seem to get as much pleasure from the visit as the prisoners themselves. All it needs is someone to ask them. Any "live" warden or jailer can easily provide some form of recreation once a week. In the very small places it may not be possible, but in the majority of them it will be found comparatively easy, and even in the smaller places perhaps some organization like Community Service, which, I believe, is the present name for the War Camp Community Service, would gladly undertake to furnish some entertainment once a week to the prisoners in the jails.

And when I say "recreation," I mean

something the prisoners will consider such, and not the things some well meaning persons think they should enjoy. When, during a recent penitentiary investigation, I called attention to the absence of any recreation, the chaplain arose and indignantly denied my statement, contending that they held both church services and sabbath school every Sunday.

Do not think such recreation is "pampering" prisoners. Confinement in a penal institution is sufficient punishment in itself. Neither the community nor the prisoner is helped by adding to his mental and spiritual torpor in every direction save crime, and to his physical inertia, which cannot do other than undermine health. It is not a sane preparation for honest self-support.

At least reading matter could be supplied. This would be a very good way to give the prisoner something to think about besides the vainglorious tales of criminal adventure and worse related by

269

his associates. Again I think of an organization eminently fitted to carry on this work. The American Library Association, which has done such splendid things for the soldiers, sailors and merchant mariners, would find a large and worth while field if it would turn its attention toward the jails of the country. I feel sure that such an activity in their hands would become, as during the war, a matter not only of providing diversion, but of creating morale and aiding future careers.

Kangaroo courts should be stamped out entirely. Responsibility for the discipline of a jail should rest in the officials, where it belongs, and not in the prisoners. If a jailer is too lazy or indifferent to maintain discipline he is not the proper man for the place and should be removed.

I have already commented on the fact that I have personally known federal judges to be swept off their feet with astonishment when told of the frightful conditions existing in jails to which they had been sentencing prisoners for years. Because of this ignorance, no judge can know what his own sentences actually mean. Yet, as I have said previously, federal judges are frequently asked by prisoners to have their sentences changed from six months in jail to one year in the penitentiary if the prisoner happens to know the conditions existing in each. The "utter detachment of the judiciary" becomes ridiculous when it is carried to the extreme of keeping utterly aloof from knowledge of the institutions in which sentences must be served. Every judge should visit, at least once a year, each institution to which he sends prisoners, and should make these visits at unexpected times, so that the officials will not have an opportunity to "set the stage."

By all means abolish the fee system of feeding prisoners. Prisoners should be fed at actual cost and no official should get one cent of profit or compensation

271

from such feeding. As I have previously explained, under the fee system the prisoner thinks he is being exploited, and in many cases he thinks correctly. Although a sheriff or jailer be ever so conscientious, he is always open to the charge that he is making a profit from starving prisoners. In many jails where the fee system prevails prisoners are allowed to buy food with their own money. In such cases they invariably complain that they are not given enough purposely so that they will spend their own funds on the jail commissary. This charge is often false, but it is exceedingly difficult to disprove. To sum the matter up, there are dozens of reasons against the fee system and not one in its favor.

Far more disastrous to the prisoners and to society than all the evils discussed above, is that great unmitigated curse of idleness. There are perhaps anywhere from two hundred to three hundred thousand persons confined in the jails of the United States at all times.

Whether confined for a day, a month, a year, or five years, they are kept in utter and complete idleness. They are not given any kind of work, either productive or unproductive, to perform. The economic loss to the individual and to the state, the mental and physical stagnation, and the moral pollution which inevitably follow in the wake of the man who has nothing to do, daily take their relentless toll in the jails. Here, indeed, is the devil's prime ingredient. Idleness is prevalent in practically all jails, whether the one at Wichita which I have already described as being exceptionally horrible, or the one at Pittsburgh to which I have also referred as being exceptionally good.

Make the jails as modern and up-to-date as you will, equip them with all modern sanitary conveniences, have the food well balanced, sufficient and nutritious, give the prisoners plenty of air and exercise, and a decent amount of wholesome recreation, and you have not gone half the distance it is necessary to go if you would build the prisoner who still has something left in him into a useful and law abiding citizen. You must give him something to occupy his mind, something to make him feel that he is a producer and a wage earner, and not a mere thing whose services are of no use either to himself or to anyone else.

What can you expect of a man after he has spent anywhere from three months to a year alternately lying in bed, shooting crap, playing cards, getting well acquainted with the most hardened denizens of the underworld, learning the "delights" of morphine, and listening to stories of crime and adventure and worse, told always with a few home-made embellishments? But what else is there to do? The prisoner can't work because he hasn't any work to do. He cannot read, because, except in a very few jails, he gets nothing to read. He cannot think about any matter of real moment, because he has no outside stimulus. If it were only possible to obtain figures, I believe it could easily be shown that a tremendous number of the most appalling crimes are the offspring of idleness in the jails.

Thousands of prisoners would be only too glad to do some kind of work, particularly if they were given even a small compensation, and I have had prisoners actually go down on their knees to me when I was going through jails and beg and plead that they be given some kind of work to do. The question is, how is this idleness to be overcome? There are many obstacles in the way of installing industries. In the first place, the time which the average prisoner spends in any one jail is so short that by the time he learns the work it would be time for his release. In the second place it seems to be the prevailing legal opinion that prisoners awaiting trial cannot be compelled to work. In the third place, thousands of jails in the country have not a sufficient number of prisoners in confinement at any one time to justify the installation of industries. There are probably some other minor obstacles, but these three I believe are considered the main ones.

The first objection seems to present some difficulty, but even this could be lessened by a plan for consolidating seveal counties into one "judicial district" which I shall present shortly. Under this plan some industry could be selected for each "judicial district" which entirely or largely calls for unskilled labor, thus taking care of the many persons who serve short terms as well as the others. If certain phases of the industry did require some training, under my plan there would usually be a sufficient number of persons in the district serving long enough terms to perform these. However, it goes without saying that industries requiring as much unskilled labor as possible would be best. Each district will have to select an industry particularly suited to itself. The problem will require study by capable men in each state, taking cognizance of climate, and geographical and other natural considerations.

Perhaps by far the better plan would be to have the prisoners engage in farming. Of course you cannot make a farmer out of any man any more than you can make a doctor or lawyer out of him, but I think we should put aside all idea of vocational training in the jails, as the average time the prisoners remain there is entirely too short to permit the teaching of any trade. The next best thing is to give them employment at the most healthful kind of labor where they will get plenty of air and exercise, and certainly farming is as good as anything for this purpose. Three or four months of work of this kind would greatly improve the health of the thoroughly dissipated men who form the larger percentage of those confined in our jails, while it would certainly be in no way detrimental to the smaller and better class.

As to the second objection, the generally held theory that prisoners awaiting trial cannot be compelled to work, this upon closer examination appears to dissipate into thin air. When states pass compulsory work laws for men who are at liberty, it is the height of absurdity to assert that they cannot compel men to work who are in jail. But compulsory laws may not be necessary, as I believe the great majority of prisoners would be glad to work if properly compensated.

As for the third objection, I have a plan to offer which, although it may seem startling at first, will I believe go far toward solving not only all phases of the problem of idleness, but also many of the other evils to which attention has been called. I think that in every state four or five adjacent or contiguous counties should be combined into one judicial district, with one judge, one sheriff, one set of court officials and one jail. There would be, of course, some additional expense in transporting prisoners to this

278

centrally located institution, but it would be more than overcome by the saving in the salaries of judges, sheriffs, and other court attaches.

Special state legislation would, of course, accomplish this, but that certainly is not an insurmountable barrier. With over three thousand counties in the United States, each with its own court house, county judge, sheriff, clerk of court, treasurer and other county officials, there is an enormous economic waste. Where a county has only a daily average of four or five prisoners the county commissioners invariably take the view that such a small number does not justify any outlay for keeping the jail in proper condition, or building a new one when the old one has outlived its usefulness.

I do not minimize the part politics plays. In many, if not all of the states in the Union it is the greatest barrier to the betterment of jail conditions and the scientific handling of the criminal problem. It may well be that political opposition to the consolidation of counties in the manner mentioned will be found too great to overcome. In that event efforts should be made to place under state control several large jails to be erected at advantageous points throughout the state. The prisoners now scattered in the many county jails should then be concentrated in these state institutions, just as prisoners now sentenced to the penitentiary are concentrated in one or two state prisons.

Under the present system it is not possible in the majority of cases to obtain a high class man for sheriff or jailer, because the county cannot afford to pay enough money to attract a man of this type. With one place of holding court for four or five counties and with the jail located at such a place, all these objections could be met. A modern jail of fair size could be built and a high class man appointed jailer at a salary which would justify him in devoting all of his time and thought to his work. Concerning the various shortcomings of jailers and wardens, and the equipment they should bring to their posts, I have already spoken in Chapter IX.

Work of any kind should naturally carry with it a system of reasonable compensation for the prisoners. It can scarcely be expected that this compensation would be as much as that paid workers in similar occupations on the outside, but it should certainly be sufficient to permit the prisoner to accumulate a sufficient amount of money in two or three months to float himself when he gets out until he is able to obtain some work to do after his release. It is not sane to make work of any kind an unknown thing for months and even years, to take away entirely the habit of wage earning, to make impossible the saving of a little fund against the day of release for continuing the broken thread of normal life, and then expect a man or woman, all lax and unaccustomed, to immediately capture an honest livelihood in the great outside struggle of economic competition. Such a policy has as much sense as employing an incendiary in a powder mill.

Determined though a man may be to lead a straight life, it takes but a day or two of hunger to bring him to a mental state of self-justification which is the first step to crime. To turn a man out in summer under such circumstances is bad enough—in winter it is simply criminal.

Not the least of the just criticisms against our penal system is that the dependents of a prisoner suffer during his confinement more than he himself does. I believe some of this distress caused the innocent could be relieved in a measure at least by turning over to such dependents a portion. if not all, of the money which the prisoner earns, whether the prisoner himself be willing or unwilling. And unquestionably a prisoner who is subsequently acquitted should receive a greater compensation than one who is convicted. Certainly it is but a small recompense for the deprivation of his liberty and the trouble, expense, inconvenience and humiliation which his imprisonment has caused him. As the law stands at present, a man held in jail for months and then acquitted gets no compensation of any kind, although his imprisonment may have cost him many hundreds of dollars through unemployment.

One of the basic necessities for maintaining the jails in proper condition is their regular inspection by some competent authority empowered either to make necessary changes, or to recommend such changes for action by an authoritative board. A few of the States have either a board or an inspector authorized to investigate conditions. Often the boards have many other phases of work in their charge. Its members are not appointed because of any special fitness or training for penal work. They are usually political appointees and change with each administration. In some states the grand jury is the only authority empowered to make jail inspections and these inspections as a rule are utterly worthless.

Not only competence is essential, but also the legal power to make necessary changes. This power, as I said before, should be vested in the inspecting authority itself, or in some body to which such inspecting authority makes its reports. I have previously gone into some detail concerning the State Board of Michigan, which not only has authority to inspect jails but is also empowered to institute mandamus proceedings to compel the offending county to carry out its recommendations even to the extent of building a new institution. Such a law as this should be enacted in every State. It is the one way and the only way in which jails can be maintained at a high standard. Rather have no inspecting officials than those who are incompetent and no board unless it has power to enforce the making of necessary changes.

The Federal Government can solve its jail problems only by building its own institutions. Speaking generally, I think the Government takes infinitely more care of its prisoners than do the various states, but in spite of its best efforts it is hampered at every turn by having no jails of its own. All the Government can do is to request the local authorities to improve conditions. And if officials do not want to accede to such a request they simply don't. I cannot better illustrate this spirit than by giving a frequent experience of mine. Upon many occasions, on insisting to sheriffs that federal prisoners be given better quarters, I have been requested, with more or less politeness, to "tell the government to take its prisoners and go to hell with them!"

It is a disgraceful condition of affairs that the Government is forced to use many institutions which it knows are not suitable. Just as it has no jails of its own today, so in former years the Government had no penitentiaries at all. Even today it has no penitentiary for women. Women are boarded at State penitentiaries. Years ago the situation with regard to penitentiaries became intolerable and the Government was forced to build some prsions of its own. The same situation exists now with regard to jails and a prison for women, and has in fact existed for many years. Even if the institutions of the country were kept in splendid conditions, the Government should maintain jails of its own and a prison for women, as it alone should be responsible for the treatment of its prisoners.

CHAPTER XII.

ESTABLISHING A NEW ORDER.

Treating the Criminal, Not the Crime—Weeding Out the Unfit—Curing Psychic Diseases—A "Receiving Prison"—Felony Cases—Misdemeanants — The Pure Indeterminate Sentence—The "Genuine" Criminal—Punishment No Deterrent—National Identification Bureau—How It Should Function—Bureau at Leavenworth—Some Deceptive Cases—Out of the Dark Ages.

As stated in the opening chapter, in any plan to reduce crime and the number of criminals, there are two principal matters to be accomplished: one, the prevention of any conditions which tend to create, encourage or develop criminals; and two, the proper classification and appropriate treatment of offenders, including the permanent confinement of those who are shown to be incurable. The former, of which the American jail is the outstanding evil, has been dealt with. Remedies and improvements have been advanced all along the line. But for the latter no remedies or improvements can be proferred because as yet it does not even exist. The task before us in this field is the nationwide establishment of a new order of things.

Generally speaking, the only classification of criminals which exists at present is that made according to the nature of the crime, and whether it is a first or a repeated offense. The prisoner himself is not classified, nor is he therefore given any appropriate treatment which should serve to correct him and prevent a repetition of crime. Only a crude punishment —on a par with the crude classification— is meted out; a punishment which merely confines him for some time in one of our uniform institutions for the purpose, and then turns him loose on the community, often to follow his criminal tendencies again.

For it must be understood to begin with that a large percentage of recidivists is composed of the feeble-minded, the defective, the epileptic, the moron, the pervert, and the other numberless gradations of inferiority and abnormality. Mere confinement does not cure these cases. Also, modern scientific developments have demonstrated that it is quite possible to analyze and successfully treat psychic diseases as well as physical. This knowledge must be utilized for all derelicts so that the mentally unfit, those suffering from phobias, manias, and so forth, can be weeded out for asylums; the casual criminal corrected; and the incurable criminal confined for life.

I believe the ideal plan, in the light of the present development in the fields of criminology and penology is to establish in each state a "receiving prison," to which every person convicted of a felony should be sent for study by a psychiatrist and psychologist. This study should include the heredity and environment of the prisoner, his physical and mental condition, his previous arrests and sentences, his school record, and all other information concerning him which is obtainable. Reports from his parents, his associates, his teachers, the police and prison officials and such others as have come in contact with him may be obtained. If the study shows that he is a defective delinquent, he should be sent to an institution for this class; if insane, to an insane asylum; if a confirmed criminal, to prison for life; and if he is normal and has reformative possibilities, to a suitable institution for such length of time as a board, consisting of a psychologist, a psychiatrist, and one other member, either a business or professional man of intelligence and judgment, considers advisable. He should then be released, placed in a position to which he is suited, and compelled to report to a parole officer at frequent intervals. If he should subsequently be convicted again, that fact and the circumstances surrounding it should be considered as factors in determining whether or not he should be given another opportunity.

This plan would take care of those convicted of felonies. But there is still the large class of misdemeanants remaining. Because a man is convicted of a misdemeanor does not by any means say that he is not as dangerous to the community as the one convicted of a felony. As a matter of fact, large numbers of those convicted of felonies have previously been convicted only of misdemeanors, while many of those convicted of misdemeanors have previously been convicted of felonies. This situation could be met at least in part by having a psychologist and psychiatrist attached to each court having jurisdiction of misdemeanors, whose duty it would be to single out those who are a potential menace to the community, and send them to the "receiving prison" for study, to be treated as are all other prisoners sent there.

Obviously, however, these court scientists could only cull out for further study those who are patently in need of it, as they would have neither the time nor the facilities necessary to make extended investigations concerning any one prisoner.

There is actually little, if any, difference in the types of prisoners convicted of misdemeanors and those convicted of felonies. I am speaking now of misdemeanors in the strict sense, and not such minor offenses as violating traffic laws, gambling, fighting and kindred violations. In many cases the law draws an arbitrary line between a misdemeanor and a felony. For instance, any sum stolen under $50.00 may be a misdemeanor; anything over that amount, a felony. The man who steals a pocketbook and finds only $40.00 in it may well wish that he had committed a felony.

By a parity of reasoning, therefore, it would seem that those convicted of misdemeanors, as well as those convicted of felonies, should be sent to a "receiving prison." And undoubtedly they should be. But I believe it would be the better plan to get the "receiving prison" for felons into active operation first, and for the present, at least, weed out in the court room, in the manner I have indicated, those misdemeanants who are palpably in need of further study.

Under the receiving prison system, of course, the pure indeterminate sentence would necessarily exist, without minimum or maximum. Strictly speaking, it would not be a sentence at all, but merely commitment to the receiving prison, or clinic, or house of detention, or whatever it may be called, for study and disposal as outlined.

I believe that under this system the incurable, or what may be called "genuine" type of criminal will be found to constitute an important percentage. Whether he is the product of inherited tendencies or of early environment or both, this person would commit crime under any conditions. Such an individual has a talent and love of crime for crime's sake, just as a musician has a talent and performs for music's sake, or a baseball player for the game's sake. In similar fashion to other men the inherent criminal finds his strongest tendency and follows his calling. And as long as human nature remains what it is I believe that we shall have the genuine type of criminal with us to more or less extent.

Punishment, even though public, does not have a deterrent effect on the genuine criminal, and perhaps very little on the other types. I cannot better illustrate this than by the following. Years ago, in England, they hanged men for a large number of crimes, among them pocket picking. Executions were public and many thousands of people attended them. It was found that so many hundreds of persons engaged in picking the pockets of those who attended hangings for pocket picking that the authorities were forced to abandon public executions. When men pick pockets while watching others being hanged for the same offense, what little real deterrent effect punishment has can easily be seen. Therefore, it is the very pinnacle of folly to release time and again a man who has shown, according to the best scientific methods available, that he will not "go straight."

Since a complete knowledge of a prisoner's criminal record is of cardinal importance under the receiving prison plan, there should by all means be a national bureau for supplying this information. Every prisoner arrested, charged with a felony or real misdemeanor (not a trivial offense) should have his finger prints taken and a copy forwarded to this bureau. If the prisoner is subsequently acquitted this record should be destroyed, thus preventing anything that may be construed as a stigma remaining against him. The Bertillon measurements should not be taken because they are of doubtful use in the case of women and adolescents, the former because of the thick hair and the latter because of growth. And for the further reason also that the taking of such measurements requires smoe skill, while the taking of finger prints is merely mechanical, and can easily be taught to any sheriff or peace officer.

The largest bureau of this kind in the country today is the Bureau of Criminal Identification maintained by the United States Government at Leavenworth, Kansas. This Bureau has on file approximately six hundred thousand finger prints. Comparatively speaking, this is a drop in the bucket. Thousands upon thousands of prisoners are convicted of crime every year whose finger prints are never sent to the Bureau at Leavenworth. Each large city maintains a finger print bureau which is practically independent. Smaller cities and towns have none. As a result a prisoner arrested in New York may plead a first offense and receive consideration on that account, when as a matter of fact he may have been convicted of crime a dozen other times in various cities of the country.

One prisoner, for instance, with a long record back of him, escaped from the penitentiary. It happened that he subsequently was arrested in a western city charged with highway robbery. The evidence against him was slight and he probably would have been acquitted and released but for the accidental recognition of him by another offender who "squealed." If his finger prints had been taken and sent to a central identification bureau detection would have been certain and would not have depended on a pure accident.

A girl confined in an Eastern penitentiary was dealt with very leniently because she told the judge that this was her first offense. On investigation, I found that, despite her apparent youth, she was twenty-four years old and had a six years' record of crime.

But if there was one central identification bureau and every police chief and sheriff in the United States were compelled by law to take the finger prints of all prisoners of the classes mentioned and to send such finger prints to the central identification bureau, a complete record could be kept of the number of times a prsioner had been convicted. So that, if an official in Seattle arrested a man charged with highway robbery, and the finger print record of the central bureau showed that he had been convicted once in Tampa, Florida, and once in Buffalo, N. Y., that fact could be reported back to the Seattle officers and made known to the "receiving prison" officials.

The increasing general interest being taken in all matters pertaining to crime and criminals is an encouraging sign, and one which indicates that after the many centuries of alternate official cruelty and sentimentality in dealing with the problem, mankind is at last awakening to the fact that if it would even protect itself, it must approach such a tremendous subject on a purely rational, scientific basis. Foul dungeons do not make decent citizens. As I have said, I believe the principal reason for our unspeakably vile jail conditions to be, not that the public is indifferent, but that it is not informed. I have endeavored, therefore, to bring home the fact that, relics of the dark ages as they are, such conditions do exist, and not in occasional instances but in almost every jail in America. The opinion has been expressed that once the public became cognizant of this barbarous situation, it would demand a swift change.

I have given the facts. Will the remedy be applied?

THE END.